THE ART OF SELLING
A Scientific Approach

THE ART OF SELLING
A Scientific Approach

NEIL J. BINDER

NICE IDEA
PUBLISHING
•
NEW YORK, NEW YORK

ISBN 0-9679249-1-X

1.Business   2. Real Estate   3. Self Help   4. Psychology

Published by Nice Idea Publishing, Inc.
352 Park Avenue South
New York, NY 10010

Acknowledgments

First and foremost, I would like to thank all the salespeople who have gone through the Bellmarc Training Program. Without their continued confusion, my own clarity would be much diminished. It was truly a mutual learning experience.

I would also like to thank my business partner, Marc Broxmeyer, who continued to encourage me to go out of the box and create ideas that on some occasions were utterly bizarre. It was Marc more than anyone who encouraged me to join him in various workshops and courses that helped me find interesting solutions to some of my most perplexing problems.

A critical cog in any good book is the editor. I have been greatly blessed by having the assistance of Betsy Malcom. Betsy remained ruthless to the end and made me face realities about the quality of my writing that I am still suffering with. She truly is an author's best friend.

Finally, I would like to thank Nina Scerbo, who not only designed this book, including the cover, but also helped me through all the emotional anguish of putting it together.

To the memory of
Dr. Abraham Martin Binder

Contents

Introduction

My background is in real estate sales, but this is not just a real estate sales book — the principles apply to selling any product, service or idea.

For more than 20 years I have been the co-owner of the Bellmarc Companies, one of the largest residential real estate brokerage firms in New York City, and in this capacity I dedicate a significant portion of my time to teaching new sales associates. Initially, I believed that selling meant communicating knowledge, that if trainees knew the fundamentals of real estate they would be able to sell it, but I was wrong. Some well-trained salespeople did poorly, while others with less knowledge became successful. What was the key?

I searched for answers through reading, workshops and my own experience. Then I tested strategies on trainees during my weekly seminars in order to see which were effective. In time, successful techniques emerged, forming the foundation for future lessons. The format for this book is that of a training session. I suggest that you envision yourself being a student in a class and that you participate in the experience.

I have discerned some overall truths that I think apply to any kind of selling:

• YOU ARE NOT IN A PERSONAL RELATIONSHIP WITH YOUR CUSTOMER; YOU ARE IN A BUSINESS RELATIONSHIP. Don't ever rely on a personal relationship to substitute for good service. A customer has the right to go where he will be best served for the least amount of money. You have the right to make a profit and further your own goals.

• YOU DO NOT BUILD A BUSINESS BY MAKING ANY ONE SALE. The customer must want to do business with you again and recommend you to others. The initial sale is the beginning, not the end, of the relationship.

• GOOD SALESPEOPLE LOVE TO SELL. If you don't, pretend with all your heart that you do. If you love your work, customers will respond to your enthusiasm. If you don't, they will know that too.

• HUNGRY SALESPEOPLE STARVE. Always remain in control. Don't ski straight down the mountain because it's the shortest way — take stock of the terrain and adjust your course accordingly. Be observant and flexible and keep building momentum as you move toward a deal.

• DON'T LIVE FOR YOUR BUSINESS. Talking about a product is not enough to make a lasting relationship with a customer. If you want to succeed in sales, have a life beyond selling.

• YOU NEED AN INNER PARTNER. Whether it's God or a person in your mind, you must talk to someone who will really hear the truth. Your inner partner will comfort you, believe in you and protect you from yourself.

You won't see these principles mentioned again in this book because they form the departure point for our journey.

A great salesperson looks at selling as merely another aspect of a full life. The joy of helping people find what they need and the satisfaction that comes from being an integral part of that decision is the essence of greatness for a salesperson. Thus, economic gain is merely a byproduct of the whole process.

When I talk to my personnel director about hiring new applicants, I generally set up a number of simple criteria for her to evaluate. First, the salesperson must be intellectually capable. Second, the salesperson must make a full-time commitment. And third, you must like him. We never look at a résumé, and prior knowledge of the industry is meaningless. What's really important is, Would I like to buy something from you?

AUTHOR'S NOTE: *The use of the masculine form throughout this book is intended to apply to both males and females.*

CHAPTER I

Growing Through Confusion

The first step in selling is understanding your customer. You must open your mind fully to what he says and how he says it. To do this, you must go beyond your own experience. You must become confused.

PERCEPTIONS OF REALITY

We all have preconceived ideas about other people that affect our dealings with them. We judge them on the basis of our own experience. Based on that, we predict how things will work and what people will do.

> Donna, what kind of home do you think Joan wants to buy?
> DONNA: *"I'd have to ask her."*
> You would? Why? Don't you have a sense of what you would want if you were her?
> DONNA: *"Yes, I could look at her and draw conclusions. I'd say she would want a two-bedroom on the Upper East Side in a doorman building. Something very classy."*

See, with no frame of reference except her own experience and observation, Donna determined what Joan would want. She has made a lot of assumptions, hasn't she? But we all do it. The problem is, these are often false conclusions.

⁐ FILTERING INFORMATION

To compound the problem, even when Donna gets information about Joan, she filters it. She may generalize, distort or delete part of it to make it fit neatly within her map of the world. You do this as well.

If I tell you, "Black doesn't look good on you — you shouldn't wear it," you may generalize and say, "Neil has no taste," or even, "Men have no taste." You may distort my statement to fit your preconceptions and say: "Neil doesn't mean that black doesn't look good on me. He must have a problem, and he's taking it out on me!" You may even delete the entire thing, regard it as unimportant and say, "Oh, how are you today?" without even thinking about what I said. We all filter what we hear in some way to make it conform to our preconceptions.

⁐ DEVELOPING A STRATEGY FOR LEARNING

When you are meeting a new customer and want to understand his needs, your mind immediately begins its filtering routine. Your first challenge is to minimize this and maximize the amount of clear data coming in. You must go beyond your own experience to understand your customer. Think of new information as white light, and you are wearing a blue filter over your eyes. The incoming light will seem blue until the filter is removed. To remove the filter, you must take in and process the new information and then integrate it into your thinking without regard to your own beliefs and assumptions.

If you receive new data without filtering it through your preconceptions, you create a new block to add to the wall of blocks built from your experience. If you filter the new information, you solidify your beliefs at the expense of learning something new.

❧ CONFUSION AS AN OBJECTIVE

The key to removing the filter is to create a starting place where there are no preconceived notions, not even of right and wrong or good and bad. You do this by getting confused. When you are confused, you ask questions. You might ask: "What does that mean? Why is he doing that? What's going on?" That's confusion!

You get confused in order to learn without preconceptions — to see new information clearly and become open to new ideas. If you take in new information in a state of confusion, you can integrate it as growth.

❧ LEARNING HOW TO BE CONFUSED

Confusion is a state of learning. If you think you already know the answer, you are not open to learning. If you are confused, you will seek knowledge.

This exercise should help you understand how to get confused. Write down what you would say in the following situations:

First, say I knock on your front door and you open it and see me.

Second, you are sitting at your desk and I come up to you.

What were your responses?

MAUREEN: *"What do you want?"* and *"How can I help you?"*

DAVE: *"Hi, what are you doing here?"* and *"Hi, how are you?"*

SUSAN: *"Hi, I'm surprised to see you"* and *"Good morning, Neil. How are you?"*

STEVE: *"Hi, what can I do for you?"* and *"Hi, how are you doing?"*

I didn't say you couldn't respond the same way in both situations, but in every case the words you chose were different. I have done this exercise many times, and each time a different visual cue elicits a different response.

Now let's say I stop by your desk, and you tell me what you would have said had I appeared at your home. In other words, mix up the responses and the situations. As I arrive at your desk, what are you going to say?

[Neil gets each person to envision the response to the second experience with his or her first statement.]

This response was appropriate, but how did it feel?

SUSAN: *"It just wasn't right. I don't know, it was...."*

MAUREEN: *"I don't understand. I'm confused about it."*

DAVE: *"It doesn't sound right to me. I would use the other words."*

Something is out of kilter. You can't take words out of one context and put them in another — you are violating clear lines of order in your brain when you do. When you try to mesh the two scenarios, your mind doesn't understand the resulting combination. It wants to re-sort and restore internal consistency.

Confusion is as much a state of mind as happiness or sadness is. If I tell a joke, and you laugh, the joke has stimulated the state of happiness. I want you to stimulate the state of confusion, so that you can learn how to access it when you need to. Your disorientation is a means to reorientation and growth.

HOW THE MIND CLASSIFIES AND CATEGORIZES

Let's talk more about the mind's tendency to classify and categorize.

Donna, is there something you know very well?

DONNA: *"Yes, I used to be an English teacher. I know teaching."*

Is there anything that confuses you?

DONNA: *"I've always had trouble with math."*

Okay, now picture yourself teaching an English class. Make the picture clear and vivid.

DONNA: *"Okay."*

What are you wearing?

DONNA: *"A blue suit."*

What else do you see?

DONNA: *"I see myself at the blackboard talking to the class."*

Now I want you to locate that picture. Is it high or low? Left or right?

DONNA: *"Right here, in front of my face."*

[Neil records Donna's responses on the blackboard.]

Would you call that close or far?

DONNA: *"Close."*

Is it big or small?

DONNA: *"Small."*

Is it in color or black and white?

DONNA: *"Black and white."*

What shape is it?

DONNA: *"It's square and kind of fuzzy around the edges."*

Okay, this list is *Something You Know*:

Something You Know
- Front — face high
- Close
- Small
- Black and white
- Square
- Fuzzy

Does that describe the picture, or is something missing?

DONNA: *"That's it."*

Good. Now erase it from your mind and concentrate on a new picture. Picture yourself doing math. That picture will be *Something Confusing*. Can you tell me about it?

DONNA: *"I am studying the training material and doing one of the math problems. I am wearing the same suit I have on today."*

Where is the picture located?

DONNA: *"It's way over on the left."*

Is it near or far?

DONNA: *"Very far."*

Is it large or small?

DONNA: *"Pretty small."*

Smaller or larger than the picture you looked at before?

DONNA: *"Smaller."*

Is it in color or black and white?

DONNA: *"Black and white."*

Can you tell me its shape?

DONNA: *"It's round and fuzzy."*

Okay, this list is *Something Confusing*:

Something Confusing
- Left
- Very far
- Smaller
- Black and white
- Round
- Fuzzy

You mentally locate Something You Know in one area and Something Confusing in a different place. Each concept has a different shape, size and quality. Now, let's take this a step further.

Donna, take that picture of Something You Know — the one of you teaching the English class — and shrink it down to the size of a dot.

Now, flip the dot around. On the back of the dot, put the picture of you doing math, Something Confusing, and start making it bigger. However, make it stay in front of your face, and give it all the other features associated with Something You Know. How do you feel about it now?

DONNA: *"Better."*

What is better about it?

DONNA: *"I don't know, it just feels better. I feel like I understand it and I am more sure about what to do."*

Isn't that weird? Change the location and other contextual features of the picture, and bingo! New feelings. New clarity. New results.

❧ CONFUSION AS A MENTAL CATEGORY

An experience is confusing because it has been categorized that way by your brain. It is as if your mind were a library in which experiences are registered in different mental states that are located in distinct sections of the room. You could reposition an experience to the area where you keep things you understand, the area of Something You Know. The result would be different feelings and a greater sense of clarity and comprehension. However, this is not the section for learning. To learn more, you must enter another area: Confusion.

In Confusion, your mind is a sponge, searching for more information in order to give you new awareness. To learn what your customer wants, you must do more than listen — you must get confused. What your customer says must not go into the section of Something You Know, but into the section *What You Don't Know but Want to Find Out:*

Confusion. This does not come naturally; you must make it a conscious undertaking. It will come more easily once you know what to do.

With Confusion as your objective, you have the power to stop judging information and enjoy its possibilities. Confusion can be an amazing tool for learning and personal growth. Once you get confused and gather information, you can choose to reconsider it as something you know — learn then confirm.

✐ THE SALESPERSON JUDGMENT TRAP

Imagine entering a dark room. Your mind gropes for information. Is there a wall? Are there discernable features? As you touch everything, you learn about your surroundings. After you find a light switch, you can see where you are, and the light confirms the knowledge gained from groping in the darkness.

When you enter the next dark room, will you feel your way to explore what is there, or will you panic at the lack of clarity? You could reach for a light switch where you found one before, but what if it isn't there? How will you figure out the best way to move forward?

Some salespeople get angry and insist that the switch should be there even if it's not. They have it all figured out before they even begin and accept only information that affirms what they think they already know. They generalize, distort and delete new information until it confirms their preconceptions. These people reject the darkness that surrounds them instead of searching for light.

Customers reject such salespeople because, by their actions, they reject their customers. When I ask them: "What's going on? Why haven't you made a deal?" they never say: "It's my fault. I don't know something I need to know." They always say, "It's the market," "It's the company," "Buyers are idiots," "Sellers are jerks." When I ask if they should consider changing their approach, they get angry. They say I don't understand their situation. This is true, yet I also see that they are not confused enough. Their lack of confusion limits their ability to learn about their customers and see new avenues of opportunity.

Some very successful salespeople have it all figured out. They are not confused. They put all their chips on one clear strategy, and they win. They are so intense that they feel if they do not succeed they will die. They do well because their very lives are at stake.

When I talk to these people about Confusion, they love it! However, they are so connected to what they know that they can't get out of their own world to learn about alternatives. They talk about Confusion, but they aren't open enough to use it. While they are successful salespeople, they don't reach their full potential in business or in life.

The best salespeople are always confused and seeking knowledge. They view everyone they talk to as a source of information and integrate what they learn. They get all the information they can from the customer before making a proposal based on what the customer reveals. These people don't waste time judging or getting depressed. They realize that there is no bad news, only a confusing situation that must be analyzed and explored until new information opens up new choices. The best salespeople work very hard to stay confused — and profit greatly.

Socrates once said, "The only true wisdom is in knowing you know nothing." He understood that wisdom comes from starting with nothing and permitting everything to enter.

❧ REMAINING ISSUES

> **ANDREW:** *"'Confusion' has a negative connotation. Wouldn't it be better to use another word?"*
>
> I prefer the term Confusion because it is an active state — you are actively searching for meaning from disparate

parts. Words like "open" or "unbiased" are too passive.

The quest for unfiltered information must be an active one.

BRIAN: *"When you meet a new customer, isn't confidence and clarity more important than Confusion?"*

Becoming confused is a technique to maximize learning so you can better understand your customer's needs. If you were in your customer's position, would you prefer a salesperson who was open to everything you said and sought to fully understand what you wanted or one who thought he knew what you should do based on what he would do?

RICK: *"Don't you think that customers often don't know what they want, so that asking about their needs only affirms their ignorance about what they should do?"*

Taking what you know and adding to it what you learned can create a direction on what to teach. That is one of your primary roles as a salesperson.

⚬⚬ SUMMARY

This chapter introduces *Confusion* as a part of the learning process and explores going beyond your previous experience to gather relevant new information about a customer.

DONNA: *"What does it mean to have Confusion as an objective?"*
Confusion is a state of learning. It is the state of mind in which you are most open to receiving new information and evaluating it for what it is, without tainting it with your biases or assumptions.

RENE: *"What does it mean to receive information beyond your experience?"*
Information is often filtered (generalized, distorted or

deleted) to agree with your assumptions. Information received beyond your experience is received in a confused state — when you are open to new knowledge. Then it is processed into new learning. This new information may fit your assumptions, or it may cause you to revise them. The goal is to receive the information undistorted so that it can be evaluated for what it is.

MICHAEL: *"Explain how to become confused."*

Try this exercise: First, imagine what you would say if someone you know appeared at the door to your home. Then imagine what you would say if the same person appeared at your desk at your office.

Take your first response and imagine applying it to the second experience.

You will become confused because you are mixing mental categories in your mind.

SYLVIA: *"What is the* Salesperson Judgment Trap?*"*

Salespeople fall into a trap when they look to confirm their assumptions rather than use Confusion to gather new information and learn. Because they label customers and situations, they fail to be open to receiving new information that might reveal new opportunities or alternatives.

Are Your Memories Resources or Restrictions?

A RECENT NATIONAL PUBLIC RADIO PROGRAM, "THE INFINITE MIND," ADDRESSED A LEARNING COMPULSION DISORDER CALLED "HOARDING." HOARDERS NEVER THROW ANYTHING AWAY — THEY ACCUMULATE THINGS UNTIL THEIR LIVES BECOME SO CLUTTERED WITH STUFF THAT IT LIMITS THEIR ABILITY TO FUNCTION.

WHILE HOARDERS ARE AFRAID TO THROW ANYTHING AWAY, THEY ALSO FEEL THE CLUTTER'S WEIGHT. IT CONTROLS THEIR LIVES. BUT REMOVING IT IS HARD AND PAINFUL. MOST HOARDERS WHO FINALLY REMOVE THE CLUTTER ARE SHOCKED AT THE FREEDOM THEY FEEL. THEY KNOW THEY HAVE LOST SOMETHING, BUT THEY ARE EUPHORIC ABOUT CONQUERING THEIR FEAR.

HOW MANY OF YOU ARE MENTAL HOARDERS, ACCUMULATING EXPERIENCES IN YOUR MIND THAT CLUTTER YOUR THINKING AND LIMIT YOUR CHOICES? MENTAL HOARDERS LIVE IN A ROOM SO FILLED WITH OLD BELIEFS THAT, FINALLY, NEW INFORMATION BECOMES LOST. THERE IS NO ROOM FOR IT TO ENTER.

HOW DO WE KEEP OLD IDEAS FROM PILING UP SO OVERWHELMINGLY THAT NEW INFORMATION CAN'T GET IN? BEGIN BY ACCEPTING THAT DOING THINGS AS YOU'VE ALWAYS DONE THEM CAN LIMIT YOU. WHAT WOULD HAPPEN IF YOU THREW YOUR OLD ASSUMPTIONS AWAY? WHAT WOULD YOU CHANGE? WHAT NEW OPPORTUNITIES WOULD BECOME POSSIBLE FOR YOU?

CHAPTER 2

✗

The Mental State for Selling

To sell effectively, you need to put yourself in the right mental state. You must make the customer feel your positive energy.

✗ PUTTING ON THE RIGHT MENTAL UNIFORM

I would like to talk about the right mental state for selling and give you an exercise to help you create the right mental uniform to wear when meeting a customer.

Rene, did you ever play a sport in school?
RENE: *"Yes, field hockey."*
What did you do just before you played the game?
RENE: *"Warmed up."*
And after that, did you meet with the coach? Did he attempt to motivate you?
RENE: *"Yes. The coach got us charged up to win and got everyone committed to doing her best."*
Andre Agassi was once a top-ranked tennis player, but he said he started losing because he was not mentally prepared; he lacked the right attitude to win the game.

Mental preparation is equally important in selling. If you are not mentally prepared, you cannot succeed.

Rene, do you think the mental state for selling is the same as for a team sport like field hockey?

RENE: *"I guess so."*

So you should win, dominate and overpower? Isn't that what your coach would say to motivate you?

RENE: *"Yes, that's what he would say, but I'm not sure that's what would work for a customer. I want to be on the same team as the customer, I don't want to overpower him. I am providing a service he wants, not pushing him out of the way so I can get to the ball first. I want him to trust me and listen to me."*

CREATING A CONNECTION

Let me show you an effective technique for creating a connection and building rapport.

Rene, you can be my subject for this exercise. Sit with both of your feet on the floor and your hands resting on your knees. Now think of a time when you felt *anticipation* — when you were waiting for something to occur. Picture the experience clearly in your mind.

RENE: *"Okay."*

Bring the picture closer.

Increase its size and make it brighter.

See it in color.

Make it three-dimensional and add sound.

Now I am going to press my finger on the first knuckle of your right hand and say the word "anticipation" several times. As I do that, try to register the sensation of my finger on your knuckle, focus on the word "anticipation" and see the picture simultaneously — so that the feeling, word and picture all register as one impression in your mind.

Anticipation...anticipation...anticipation...anticipation.

RENE: *"Okay."*

Good. Now picture a time when you experienced *ecstasy.* The content of the picture is private. It's your fun; enjoy it on your own.

Make the picture closer and increase its size.

Make it brighter, in color, three-dimensional and add sound.

I will now press my finger on the second knuckle of your hand and repeat the word "ecstasy" several times. Register the picture, the sensation of my finger on your knuckle and the word as one impression.

Ecstasy...ecstasy...ecstasy...ecstasy.

Have you registered the feeling, the picture and the word?

RENE: *"Yes."*

Good, now see a scene in which you felt *curiosity.*

Bring the picture closer.

Increase its size and brightness.

Make it in color, three-dimensional and add sound.

I am pressing my finger on your third knuckle. Again, register the pressure of my finger, the word "curiosity" and the picture in your mind until you have created a connection between all three.

Curiosity...curiosity...curiosity...curiosity.

You now have three different mental states registered in your mind, each associated with a word, a picture and a touch. The senses engaged — hearing, sight and feeling — are your three primary senses. (Taste and smell are less important.) They are your main means of interacting with the world and creating memories from experience.

I want you to unite these three states, *Anticipation, Ecstasy* and *Curiosity*, into a fourth mental state: *Wonderful*. As I go through each of the states that you have registered, you should recall it and combine it with the others to form a new mental and physical sensation, Wonderful. Think of it as an alloy, a marriage of different elements to create a new substance with unique qualities of its own.

Before starting this process, I need to get a methodical rhythm going in my mind — an internal beat — so that I can recall each state at a slow, rhythmic pace and process each connection comfortably. Then I'll say the three states, Anticipation, Ecstasy and Curiosity, and press my finger on the knuckle associated with each word as I say it.

I will go slowly and methodically and conclude with the new term *Wonderful*. I will repeat "wonderful" over and over again while pressing all three knuckles at the same time, connecting the feelings.

Rene, I want you to register each sensation and merge all three pictures into a combined sensation that is Wonderful.

Anticipation...anticipation...ecstasy...ecstasy...curiosity...curiosity.

Anticipation...anticipation...ecstasy...ecstasy...curiosity...curiosity.

Wonderful...wonderful...wonderful...wonderful...wonderful.

How do you feel?

RENE [Laughing]: *"Wonderful. Wonderful."*

Would you like to meet a customer now? Would you have the appropriate state of mind to build rapport?

RENE: *"Yes."*

❧ USING THE STATE OF "WONDERFUL" TO SELL

The energy you put out is very real. If you can create a positive aura, you are the person the customer will prefer. Even if you're having a bad day, if you repeat the word "wonderful" to yourself, recall the pictures you visualized today and press your three knuckles at the same time, your body will call up the mental uniform of Wonderful. Suddenly, everything is fantastic! Strange as it seems, it happens automatically.

Your customer knows that you will make money from a sale and may be antagonistic before even meeting you. If that's his starting point, you have an uphill battle. If you're in the state of Wonderful, you will exude a positive energy that won't match his preconception of your ruthlessness. In his confusion, he will look for additional information, and what he gets from you will be inviting and desirable. Your Wonderful mood will help create a connection between you that invites comfortable open conversation and rich rapport.

❧ THE VARIABLE AND FIXED COMPONENTS OF SELLING

You might ask: "Why should I change? Why shouldn't my customers change instead?" The answer is simple: Because they can find someone else to do business with — it is their choice to pay you or someone else.

Say you go to a party. If you don't like one person, you can go on to another. If you don't like him, you can go on to a third, fourth or fifth person until you find someone you want to talk to. You can choose among the various partygoers.

In sales, the scenario is reversed. The buyer chooses you; you don't choose the buyer — at least not if you want to maximize profitability. Each buyer is an opportunity, and you must please him if you want to make a sale. You have to look at the hard ones and say, "I can do this!" You can start by feeling Wonderful when you meet, then use Confusion to find out what the customer wants. That is your objective: to become Wonderful and Confused as efficiently and effectively as possible.

℘ PRETENDING TO BE IN THE RIGHT MENTAL STATE

Creating the state of Wonderful is a device for improving your business performance. You do it to increase your chance of building rapport with your customer so you can make a profit. If you do not build rapport, the buyer will choose another salesperson, and the money will not go to you. It does not matter if the state of Wonderful is real or not — it works, and it is an effective business strategy.

I once met a psychologist who told me his objective was to have his patients pretend to be well and then convince them to pretend forever. It's okay to pretend to feel Wonderful even if you don't. Your mind does not understand the difference and neither will your customer.

℘ THE MENTAL STATE OF SELLING

Another mental uniform that will help you is the state of *Selling*. It is composed of *Deliberateness*, *Flirtatiousness* and *Humor*.

As before, I will give you an exercise to instill the state of Selling. This time, however, I will present a picture for each word, and you should focus on the feelings the pictures evoke. You will also need a sensory act, like pressing the knuckles in the last exercise, to associate with the pictures and feelings so that the three primary senses are once again invoked. Hold your thumb and succeeding two fingers.

The first element of Selling is Deliberateness. Imagine that you are walking down an empty street and see a $10 bill. Picture yourself picking it up without hesitation, and notice your feelings as you do so. Create the scene in your mind.

Make it closer, bigger, brighter and add color.

Make it three-dimensional and add sound.

Connect this picture with the word "deliberateness" and the physical sensation of holding your thumb. See the picture, listen to the word and hold your thumb.

Deliberateness...deliberateness...deliberateness...deliberateness.

Next is Flirtatiousness. Picture yourself meeting someone you are immediately attracted to. You want to get to know him, and to signal that the next step is his and that you want him to take it.

Make the picture closer...bigger...brighter...in color...three-dimensional...and add sound.

Identify it in your mind with the word "flirtatiousness" and hold your index finger.

Flirtatiousness...flirtatiousness...flirtatiousness...flirtatiousness.

See the picture, feel the feelings, listen to the word and hold your index finger so that all the sensations become associated in your mind.

The next state is Humor. Someone is laughing; you have said something funny because you are in that kind of mood. Picture a time when you made people laugh, and notice how you felt.

Make the picture closer...bigger...brighter...in color...three-dimensional...and add sound.

Identify the picture and feelings with the word "humor" and hold your middle finger.

Humor...humor...humor...humor.

Now you have registered three states: Deliberateness, Flirtatiousness and Humor. To create the alloy state of Selling, begin by recalling each of them. Start with Deliberateness — see the picture, listen to the word and hold your thumb to draw out those feelings. Now do the same for Flirtatiousness and then Humor.

Now put them together. Remember to listen to my words, recall the pictures and hold all three fingers at the same time:

Deliberateness...deliberateness...flirtatiousness...flirtatiousness...humor...humor.
Deliberateness...deliberateness...flirtatiousness...flirtatiousness...humor...humor.
Selling...selling...selling...selling.

Now notice how you feel. The people around you are dancing. You set the tune. They are smiling and conforming to your rhythm. Selling is truly a dance. You can keep people dancing to the fun and flirty tune that you choose and control. This is the mind-set of a great salesperson!

DIANE: *"When do you use the state of Selling?"*
Subliminally, it should always be there. If you falter, touch your fingers together and elicit this state in your mind.

✐ REMAINING ISSUES

CAROL: *"I can't create a mental picture. Is something wrong?"*

Not necessarily; not all people process the same way. You don't actually need to create a picture to register the desired state. If you pretend to create a picture, your subconscious will be aware of the message you are sending and register the state so that it can be recalled. The fundamental objective is to be able to recall the state of Wonderful and the state of Selling.

RENE: *"When you meet a new customer, isn't it more important to present a professional image than to be in the state of Wonderful?"*

Looking and acting professional does not preclude feeling Wonderful. You have to show the customer your personal qualities in addition to presenting the right mental state.

JANE: *"Aren't you just saying that a salesperson should be nice?"*

Yes, but there are different kinds of nice. I could be nice and sympathetic. I could be nice and humorous. You want to be the kind of nice that initiates learning and sharing.

I knew a very attractive woman who tried to sell by flirting with her male customers. She was nice, but the men weren't focusing on buying her product — the sale became a side issue. She would have been more effective if she were nice in a way that satisfied the customer's purchasing needs. She lost sales because people didn't take her seriously — she was nice in the wrong way.

JOHN: *"If your sales efforts are not going well, will the state of Selling get you back on track?"*

Not necessarily. You have to step back and identify the ingredients of what went wrong. Your state of mind is just one component of the sales process.

✎ SUMMARY

This chapter focuses on the importance of your mental state in selling. You must consciously prepare yourself to meet your customer and engage in the art of selling.

> RENE: *"Why is it important to have the right mental state?"*
> A salesperson must make a connection with the customer and create the right atmosphere for learning and building trust. The right mental state helps you do that.
>
> DIANE: *"What if you do not consciously get into the right mental state?"*
> Then you run the risk of communicating with the customer in an unappealing way. This may limit the quality of your relationship, or the customer may take his business to another salesperson.
>
> DIANE: *"What is the right mental state for meeting a customer?"*
> You want to recall the state of *Wonderful* before meeting a new customer. Touching three knuckles, recalling the pictures and feelings and repeating the word "wonderful" can invoke this state.
>
> ROBERT: *"Why do the exercises in this chapter connect a touch, a picture and a sound to each mental state?"*
> You experience the world mostly through the senses of feeling (kinesthesia), hearing and sight. Connecting all of these to one mental state firmly roots it in your mind so that it can be recalled later.
>
> CAROL: *"How is the state of Wonderful different from the state of Selling?"*
> The mental state of Wonderful is used to build rapport at the onset of a relationship. The state of *Selling* helps you gain direction and control so you can sell most effectively.

You Only Win if You Play to Win...

MY TENNIS INSTRUCTOR RECENTLY SAID, "NEIL, YOU ARE NOT GOING TO THE BALL; YOU ARE HOPING THE BALL WILL COME TO YOU!" HE INSISTED THAT I GO TO EVERY BALL, EVEN THOSE THAT WOULD HIT ME IN THE NOSE IF I DIDN'T MOVE.

WHEN I DID WHAT HE ASKED, I STARTED HITTING THE BALL WITH GREATER ASSURANCE, AND MY MIND STAYED CENTERED. I NEVER PLAYED SUCH GOOD TENNIS, AND THE ONE-HOUR LESSON PASSED AS IF IT WERE ONE MINUTE.

AT THE END OF THE HOUR, I WAS TIRED BUT ALERT. I HAD ACHIEVED A FLOW IN WHICH EVERYTHING WAS WORKING. I MADE THE EFFORT TO STAY ON MY TOES, NEVER LET MYSELF GET BORED AND NEVER LET MYSELF GET ANXIOUS. I JUST PLAYED THE GAME AS IF, AT THAT MOMENT, IT WERE MY LIFE.

CHAPTER 3

⊲

Strategies for Creating Rapport

In building rapport, you must focus on validating the customer and initiating reciprocity. This will create an atmosphere of trust conducive to exchanging information.

ℳ UNDERSTANDING SELFISHNESS

Developing rapport begins by recognizing that every individual has a distinct point of view that can be fully revealed only when each side feels well connected to the other in communication.

In order to fully appreciate an alternative viewpoint, you must recognize that everyone is selfish all of the time. Even charity is selfish, since it fulfills a need to feel good about yourself. That doesn't make the act ungenerous, just not without personal gain. Selfishness can therefore be expressed in different forms. At one end of the spectrum is the *Hedonistic Self*, characterized by anger and demand and statements like "You'd better or else." An extremely *Hedonistically Selfish* person would try to acquire sensory fulfillment, possessions and power over others. At the other end of the spectrum is the *Altruistically Selfish* person exemplified by Mother Teresa and characterized by words like "I understand" and "I want to help you." This person aspires to be internally happy and spiritually fulfilled.

Envision a line with the Hedonistic Self at one end and the Altruistic

Self at the other. In the middle is the *Hybrid Self*. A diagram of the spectrum would look like this:

The Spectrum of Selfishness

Hedonistic Self   Hybrid Self   Altruistic Self

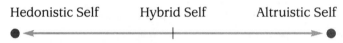

The Hybrid Self is like a game of Ping-Pong. The ball goes back and forth between Altruistic Self and Hedonistic Self. Words like "and yet," "and then," "in addition to" and "however" are shifting devices that send the conversational ball from one end of the spectrum to the other. You can use this to direct conversation away from confrontation or indecisiveness toward an effective exchange of information.

⋘ HEDONISTIC SELF TO HEDONISTIC SELF

Rita, you be a real estate salesperson, and Sylvia, you be a house seller. I want you each to communicate with the other as an extremely Hedonistic Self. Don't be yourself. Pretend to be someone you can envision acting this way.

Sylvia, let's pretend that you are asking $800,000 for your home. You need $800,000 to buy your next home, and you know the market is appreciating. You also feel that brokers are looking only to take advantage of you — they don't care; they just want to get their money. Rita, you want to make this deal — your buyer has offered $600,000, which you believe to be fair.

Now, let's play out the negotiation with both of you at the Hedonistic Self extreme.

> RITA: *"Hi, Sylvia, this is Rita Worth calling from Bellmarc. Do you have a minute to talk to me?"*

SYLVIA: *"Sure."*

RITA: *"I have great news. I have a buyer willing to pay a great price for your property."*

SYLVIA: *"Really? What did she offer?"*

RITA: *"$600,000. I think that's really a great offer, and I encourage you to accept it."*

SYLVIA: *"Rita, I'm not interested in $600,000! I told you $800,000."*

RITA: *"You never really thought that was realistic, did you? $600,000 is fabulous! I thought you would be jumping up and down!"*

SYLVIA: *"Well, I'm not. $600,000 is not even viable."*

RITA: *"Sylvia, I worked really hard to get you this buyer, and I know she is serious. This is a good price, and I think you should take it. Houses like yours don't sell for $800,000."*

SYLVIA: *"I know homes are selling for $800,000 in this area. Don't play games. If you can't do your job properly, don't make it my fault. I told you what I want, and I am selling my home on my terms, not yours. If you can't produce a good buyer, maybe I should get a competent broker. Obviously you're not one!"*

RITA: *"I did the best job of any broker in New York! You are crazy if you think you can get $800,000. Do you hear me? Crazy!"*

SYLVIA: *"Who are you to talk to me like that?"*

RITA: *"I'm an expert. I do this for a living."*

SYLVIA: *"You, an expert? I live here. I know what my home is worth. How dare you! You're looking to take advantage of me."*

Okay, we can stop here. What feelings were evoked by this conversation?

JOHN: *"Tension and anger. Voices were high-pitched. They were both antagonistic and defending themselves against the other's accusations."*

ANDREW: *"They were matching behavior. Both seemed to go to the same emotional state with increasing levels of intensity."*
SYLVIA: *"Yes, I felt myself getting caught up in the anger and defending myself."*

How many times have you been in arguments in which you ended up saying things you later regretted? That's because the matching of behavior actually put you into a kind of trance. When Sylvia and Rita started to match their behavior patterns, they formed a single hypnotic rhythm.

RITA: *"I found myself getting angry and didn't even know what I was saying. I just kept talking."*

The interesting part of this behavior is that it eventually leads to *Blowout*, a complete reversal from the Hedonistic state to the Altruistic state. The antagonism builds to such a crescendo that somebody starts giving. Then the other person reciprocates, and the emotional energy reverses.

Sylvia, did you feel any particular sensation or pressure during the conversation?

SYLVIA: *"Yes, I felt a pressure in my chest."*

Like you wanted to push Rita away?

SYLVIA: *"Yes!"*

A lot of people tell me this. They feel a strong pressure in the chest as if they were pushing the other person away.

RITA: *"I was more aware of feelings in my head. I felt kind of 'hotheaded.'"*

Each person is unique. The important thing is that you had a physical sensation that you can identify. This can be your signal in the future. It can tell you that you are being your Hedonistic Self and so is the person you are talking to.

Hedonistic Self to Hedonistic Self makes both parties defensive and builds tension. While there may be matching of behavior in which both sides feel a sense of connection, it does not create a free flow of information constructive for learning and growing. It is not an effective way to build rapport.

✐ HEDONISTIC SELF TO ALTRUISTIC SELF

The Altruistic Self wants to be caring and sensitive and do whatever the other person wants. He would give you the shirt off his back, which the Hedonistic Self would readily take.

Let's use the same setup for another exercise. The seller wants $800,000, and the buyer is offering $600,000. John, you be the Hedonistic seller, and Mary, you be an Altruistic broker submitting the offer.

MARY: *"Hi, John, this is Mary from Bellmarc. I hope I'm not disturbing you."*

JOHN: *"No. What do you want?"*

MARY: *"John, I received a bid on your home for $600,000. I know it's not enough, but I want you to tell me how you want me to proceed."*

JOHN: *"Of course it's not enough. Didn't you tell them that?"*

MARY: *"I did, and I'm sorry. I know you want more."*

JOHN: *"Why are you telling me this? It's your job to get more; go do it!"*

MARY: *"I really want to, and I know you deserve it. I am anxious to be of service."*

JOHN: *"Then stop playing games and get a buyer willing to pay me $800,000!"*

MARY: *"I know you're right, and I want you to believe that you are my top priority."*

JOHN: *"You bet I'm right. You must be incompetent!"*

MARY: *"I really am sorry. Whatever you want me to do, I'll do."*

Okay, let's stop. John, was this conversation productive?

JOHN: *"I guess so. I felt in control and that Mary was going to do what I wanted."*

True, but was there a useful give and take of information?

Did conversation flow back and forth comfortably?

JOHN: *"No, I felt like Mary should do what I wanted or else."*

MARY: *"I felt totally intimidated. I could hardly talk and didn't know what to say."*

John, did you feel any sensation?

JOHN: *"I felt like I was striking Mary on the head with a rod."*

Mary, did you feel any sensation?

MARY: *"Yes, mine was the same as John's, except that it was me being hit on the head. I felt like I was being struck."*

These are common sensations for people who perform this exercise, and they are easily distinguished from the sensations of people communicating as Hedonistic Self to Hedonistic Self. These distinctions are important. They can help you understand what's really going on in a conversation by recognizing how you feel.

In Hedonistic Self to Altruistic Self, the Hedonistic Self demands servility and action rather than an exchange of information or ideas. The Altruistic Self is prevented from educating and persuading. The Altruistic salesperson becomes an order taker rather than a source of information helping the customer make a wise decision.

JOHN: *"I don't understand. If a salesperson says, 'May I be of service?' is he not doing a good job?"*

It depends on the kind of sale.

If you own a hot dog stand and I want a hot dog, your job is to fill my order. This is *Master-Servant Selling*.

If I enter a department store and the salesperson presents a limited number of choices from which I may make a selection, this is *Counter-Selling*. The salesperson need not be overly persuasive or create an ongoing relationship. The role requires limited advice and information.

In *Persuasive Selling*, the customer is seeking information from outside sources, particularly the salesperson, before making a purchase. The salesperson chooses which items to present, describes the advantages and disadvantages of each and assists the customer in resolving issues. Thus the salesperson is integral to the decision-making process.

In Master-Servant or Counter-Selling, it may not matter if the customer is in Hedonistic Self and the salesperson is in Altruistic Self. Exchanging information and building rapport are not essential to creating the sale. However, to make a Persuasive Sale, you must communicate information effectively and develop a relationship of trust with the customer. Hedonistic Self to Altruistic Self does not encourage such communication.

MARY: *"In the book* Winning Through Intimidation, *the author says that you can sell effectively by intimidating the customer. What do you think?"*

You are talking about the salesperson being a Hedonistic Self with an Altruistic Self customer. There are limited conditions when this could work.

Sometimes a customer will ask you to "tell me what to do." If I had a serious illness, I might say that to my doctor. However, a number of prerequisites must be met before you can play Hedonistic Self successfully. Either you must be extremely reputable in the eyes of the customer, and he must be so insecure that he yearns for guidance, or the customer must view the product as so unique and valuable that he will submerge his ego to acquire it.

For example, if you were selling a property for a price I viewed as undervalued, I might accept your abusive behavior to reach the larger goal of buying on favorable terms. However, as a customer, would you feel good about subordinating yourself to a salesperson? No. You would prefer to be persuaded by an exchange in which your point of view and the salesperson's were aired openly and honestly.

Hedonistic Self to Altruistic Self fails to build rapport. One person dominates the other in an unequal communication.

❦ ALTRUISTIC SELF TO ALTRUISTIC SELF

John, you play the same broker as Altruistic Self, and Maureen, you be an Altruistic Self seller.

> JOHN: *"Hi, Mrs. Martin, this is John Smith from Bellmarc. Do you have a minute?"*
> MAUREEN: *"Of course, John. How can I help you?"*
> JOHN: *"Mrs. Martin, the buyer I brought to your home loved it."*
> MAUREEN: *"I am thrilled! Thank you for your effort."*
> JOHN: *"You're welcome. The buyer offered to pay $600,000, and I told him I would tell you."*
> MAUREEN: *"John, you're the professional, what should I do?"*
> JOHN: *"I'm at your service, Mrs. Martin. Let me know what you want, and I will be happy to accommodate you."*
> MAUREEN: *"I know you will, John, and I'm sure you care about protecting me. I'm impressed with your professionalism."*
> JOHN: *"Thank you. Your home is lovely, and it's worth a lot."*
> MAUREEN: *"John, I'm eager to see you do the deal. I know you have been working very hard."*

Okay, let's stop. Maureen, what did you think?

MAUREEN: *"It was frustrating and going nowhere. We were circling around waiting to wrestle, but no one made the first move."*

JOHN: *"We were passing each other by without ever connecting."*

Consider a husband and wife who dearly love each other. The husband says, "I love my wife so much that nothing is important except making her happy." The wife says, "I love my husband so much that I want whatever he wants." They each do only for the other, until finally, they argue — and each accuses the other of being ungrateful.

After the dust settles, both redouble their efforts until another fight occurs, bigger than the last. Finally, they go to a marriage counselor, who says: "Forget about what the other person wants. *What does each of you want?*" Their relationship only then starts to move in a productive direction.

In Altruistic Self to Altruistic Self, the desire for progress and for someone to take charge builds until the communication is no longer calm and natural; it becomes intense and raging, causing Blowout to Hedonistic Self.

Do you think Altruistic Self to Altruistic Self is effective?

SYLVIA: *"Only if you never want to get the point."*

I agree. Without direction your path goes nowhere.

Altruistic Self to Altruistic Self creates frustration because neither party states his own needs, thereby preventing those needs from ever being satisfied.

〽 HEDONISTIC SELF TO HYBRID SELF

In Hybrid Self, you first speak in Altruistic Self and then in Hedonistic Self, moving between the two like a Ping-Pong ball going from one side of the table to the other. Sylvia, you be the Hedonistic Self seller, and Ron, you play the Hybrid Self broker.

In this exercise, you should fight for your position. Don't give up. We want to examine the process, not reach a successful conclusion.

RON: *"Hi, Sylvia. This is Ron Singer from Bellmarc Realty. Do you have a minute?"*

SYLVIA: *"Yes, Ron. What do you want?"*

RON: *"I have an offer on your apartment of $600,000."*

SYLVIA: *"What? $600,000? That's ridiculous! I am absolutely not interested. What's wrong with you? Can't you do your job?"*

RON: *"Yes, this offer is awful. I am convinced your apartment is worth much more. I truly agree with everything you said, however I'm sure you understand that I have an obligation to tell you about any offer I receive. Besides, the buyer may be testing your flexibility and may be willing to come up. Why not look at this as a beginning point?"*

SYLVIA: *"You must be kidding. Don't play games with me. This is my home; there is no fire sale here! My property is worth $800,000, and I'm not playing any games to get it."*

RON: *"I think you're right. It is inappropriate to play games with something as important as your home. This is serious business, and only something much closer to $800,000 would be serious. This offer is too low. And yet this man can afford to pay your price. He is being careful because he is afraid of making a mistake. I don't blame him for acting cautiously. Let me try to get him to bid more aggressively."*

SYLVIA: *"He must come up. I am willing to listen to another offer if he is really serious. But I am not going to be taken advantage of, either by him or by you."*

RON: *"You're wise to be cautious and careful. I'll tell him that you are willing to listen to reason. However, a serious offer must be much higher. And I know you will also be sensitive to his point of view. He, too, wants to be sure that he is paying a fair price. I'm sure you understand."*

Okay, let's stop here. Sylvia, how did you feel about this conversation?

SYLVIA: *"I started out being aggressive and angry, but I couldn't sustain it with Ron continually telling me I was right. I found myself calming down, accepting some level of compromise and looking at his buyer's point of view as well as my own in deciding what I was going to say."*

RON: *"I felt you getting in sync with me. Both of us were getting into the Hybrid Self role, not just me. In the exercise, I flipped between validating Sylvia and promoting the buyer's point of view, not my own personal interest. Was that right?"*

Yes, your own interest is subsumed into the buyer's because your objective is accomplished by satisfying him.

[Neil places a $10 bill in front of Ron.]

Ron, what would you say if I told you that this $10 bill is yours?

RON: *"I would wonder why."*

Yes. And you would also probably wonder what I want from you in exchange. You would feel obligated, wouldn't you? Since I gave you something, you would owe me something in return.

RON: *"Yes, that's true."*

We all believe in reciprocity and seek to reciprocate when something of value is offered. Ego gratification has value. When you validate the buyer's beliefs, he will yearn to reciprocate. Because you are affirming the customer's message, he is not threatened; he feels a sense of *owing you something.*

Validation leads to reciprocity and creates an atmosphere of cooperation. You should always make the first move and gratify the customer, then request reciprocity. Give credence to the customer's values and beliefs. For this to be effective, however, you must be sincere. This is critically important.

A department store salesperson once showed me a sweater that she said looked fabulous on me. When I tried another sweater, she loved that one too. When I looked in the mirror, however, I saw that it was too tight and that I looked like a sausage. I did not buy any sweater because the salesperson was so transparently insincere that she could not validate my judgment even in a sweater that I liked. Because I could not trust her, I rejected the products she offered.

The main point of this exercise is to demonstrate how validating the buyer's viewpoint builds rapport. Validation stimulates reciprocity, which encourages the buyer to share his ideas and listen to yours.

> **RENE:** *"At first Sylvia's voice was tense and aggressive, but as Ron used the Hybrid Self she assumed a normal tone."*
> As the Hedonistic Self she was defensive, but once her point of view was validated she no longer felt compelled to defend herself.
> **SYLVIA:** *"Will the Hybrid Self work if someone is really angry?"*
> If you start by saying, "I agree with your point of view," the buyer should calm down. Then you have a good chance of being listened to.

❧ ALTRUISTIC SELF TO HYBRID SELF

Now let's have Sylvia play an Altruistic Self seller, and John will play the Hybrid Self broker.

JOHN: *"Hi, Sylvia, this is John from Bellmarc. Do you have a minute?"*

SYLVIA: *"Yes, John, it's wonderful to hear from you. How is my favorite real estate broker?"*

JOHN: *"Fine, thank you. And how is my favorite seller?"*

SYLVIA: *"Oh, John, compliments will get you everywhere. What can I do for you?"*

JOHN: *"I just received a $600,000 offer on your home, and I want to discuss it with you."*

SYLVIA: *"John, you really do a wonderful job getting buyers in here, and I appreciate all your effort."*

JOHN: *"Why Sylvia, thank you for the compliment. Yes, I do want to make this happen. And yet you have to tell me, what are you looking for? How can I make you happy?"*

SYLVIA: *"I appreciate your wanting to make me happy, and you know that I want to do the right thing here."*

JOHN: *"I know you are considering my feelings. However, the buyer is hoping to get a response so he can decide what to do. Will $600,000 make you happy?"*

SYLVIA: *"We must consider the buyer's position. However, I cannot afford to sell for $600,000 — it won't give me enough money to move to my next home."*

JOHN: *"I know you must consider how much you need for your next home, and the buyer must accept that you cannot go below what you can afford. That is very fair."*

SYLVIA: *"I need your help on this, John. What do you think I should I do?"*

JOHN: *"I'm happy to help you, and I propose that you think about what you need and what is fair and that we make a counteroffer that satisfies both you and the buyer. I think $700,000 is a realistic price for your home. Does that give you enough money to buy your new home?"*

Okay, let's stop. Sylvia, tell me your thoughts.

SYLVIA: *"At first things were a little wishy-washy, but I found myself thinking about my own concerns instead of John's even though I was trying not to. The conversation evolved. I think it really helped when John proposed a number. I was forced to consider if that would work based on my needs."*

JOHN: *"I felt that too. I started out wondering how I could affirm your validation of me, but by the end I was validating you and quickly returning to my position."*

Yes, you both expressed your feelings, which is fundamental to effective communication.

SYLVIA: *"I felt like I was dealing with someone who was attentive and involved in making the decision with me. The Hybrid Self really drew me in."*

That is the beauty of the Hybrid Self. It gives both parties ego gratification, opening the door to reciprocity. The Hybrid Self is a powerful tool for creating rapport and forging constructive resolutions.

The key to effective selling is not to be at the service of your customer, but to communicate in a way that leads to a resolution from which everyone benefits. Everyone's point of view should be listened to and affirmed. The customer teaches the salesperson about his needs and criteria for buying, and the salesperson teaches the customer about his choices and potential opportunities.

✎ REMAINING ISSUES

SYLVIA: *"What if the customer does not like what you have to offer?"*

There is no guarantee that the customer will buy. However, you can maximize your potential for success by learning what the customer's needs are, providing useful information and educating him about opportunities he may not be aware of.

BRIAN: *"When I'm in a conversation, I don't seem to be able to analyze it. What should I do?"*

Try to create a conversational pause. Step back and analyze what's going on. Also, make a conscious effort to validate your customer, then seek reciprocity. Controlling and analyzing the conversation should be a conscious goal that you continually monitor, at least until it comes more naturally.

❧ SUMMARY

This chapter teaches you how to create rapport with your customer. It concludes that it is most effective to use the *Hybrid Self*, in which you start by validating the customer's point of view and then ask him to reciprocate by listening to your point of view. If the customer is assured that you are listening to him, and you agree that his concerns are valid, he is likely to relax, be open and reciprocate by listening to your ideas.

CAROL: *"What are the three states of selfishness?"*
Hedonistic Self, characterized by a desire for materialism and power; *Altruistic Self*, characterized by a desire for spiritual fulfillment and good feelings; and *Hybrid Self*, which alternates between the two.

ROBERT: *"Why should you use Hybrid Self?"*
Because the customer seeks validation and, if validated, will reciprocate by listening to your alternative viewpoint.

DIANE: *"What are the different kinds of selling?"*
Master-Servant Selling: In which the salesperson has little input in the decision-making process.

Counter-Selling: In which the salesperson offers the customer choices for evaluation with limited comment.

Persuasive Selling: In which the salesperson must understand the needs of the customer and offers significant advice.

SYLVIA: *"What is the expected outcome of a conversation in which both the buyer and the salesperson are acting as their Hedonistic Selves?"*

Both will defend their positions, usually with increasing intensity. Rapport will be poor, and neither side will be open to learning from the other.

RENE: *"What is the expected outcome of a conversation in which one party is Hedonistic Self and the other is Altruistic Self?"*

The Hedonistic Self dominates the Altruistic Self. Information flows only in the direction of the Altruistic Self, who is intimidated and effectively silenced.

ROBERT: *"What is the expected outcome of a conversation in which both parties are their Altruistic Selves?"*

These conversations are frustrating, since neither party takes charge or expresses his goals clearly. Little information is exchanged, and no one arrives at a decision.

DONNA: *"What is the expected outcome of a conversation in which the customer is his Hedonistic Self and you are your Hybrid Self?"*

The customer, once his viewpoint has been validated, will reciprocate by listening to what you have to say. This is the beginning of effective communication and rapport.

DIANE: *"What is the expected outcome of a conversation in which the customer is his Altruistic Self and you are your Hybrid Self?"*

Having been validated, the Altruistic Self will accept your suggestion to broaden his perspective to include personal needs and will follow your lead toward specificity.

RON: *"Why does the sales technique 'The customer is always right' have limited effectiveness?"*

It does not encourage a two-way flow of information. Each party needs to learn from the other to reach the best overall decision.

❧

Seeing It from Another Point of View

THERE ARE TWO CATS LIVING WITH FOUR MONSTERS. THE MONSTERS ARE A LARGE MALE WITH SHORT FUR ON HIS HEAD, A SLIGHTLY SMALLER FEMALE WITH LONGER FUR ON HER HEAD AND TWO EVEN SMALLER FEMALES.

THE MONSTERS HAVE GIVEN THE CATS NAMES: MITTENS, WHO HAS WHITE PAWS, AND MISCHIEF, WHO LIKES TO PLAY.

ONE DAY MISCHIEF SAYS: "THESE MONSTERS NEVER MAKE SENSE. THE OTHER DAY THE MALE LAY DOWN TO SLEEP IN THE BEDROOM. I WENT THERE, TOO, TO PROTECT HIM. SUDDENLY, I SAW A BULGE MOVING BACK AND FORTH UNDER THE BLANKET. WELL, OBVIOUSLY IT WAS A MOUSE, SO I GRABBED IT WITH MY PAWS AND BIT IT. CAN YOU BELIEVE THAT THE MONSTER GOT ANGRY AND THREW ME OFF THE BED? HOW INCONSIDERATE!"

"YES, THEY ARE PECULIAR, AREN'T THEY?" MITTENS SAYS. "I FOUND A SECRET ROOM WHERE THEY LET IT RAIN ON THEIR BODIES. I THINK IT IS A CLEANING RITUAL." "A CLEANING RITUAL?" MISCHIEF RESPONDS IN ASTONISHMENT. "WITHOUT LICKING? THAT'S DISGUSTING!" "I AGREE," MITTENS SAYS. "AND WHEN THEY ARE DONE, THEY SCRATCH THEIR TEETH WITH STICKS AND GO TO A ROOM WITH DIFFERENT FURS, WHICH THEY ATTACH TO THEIR BODIES." "CAN'T THEY GROW ONE FUR AND KEEP IT ON?" MISCHIEF ASKS. "WELL, I DON'T KNOW," MITTENS SAYS. "THEY SEEM HAPPY WHEN THEY PUT ON THEIR FURS."

MISCHIEF SHAKES HIS HEAD. "THEY'RE SO RIDICULOUS! I GUESS YOU HAVE TO THINK LIKE MONSTERS TO APPRECIATE THEIR POINT OF VIEW."

❧

CHAPTER 4

❧

Patterns of Behavior

We all have behavior patterns that indicate how we deal with the world. When a salesperson conforms to the buyer's behavior patterns, communication can be dramatically enriched. The result is a better learning environment for both parties — and a better outcome.

❧ UNDERSTANDING DIFFERENT PERSPECTIVES

A bird would talk about experience as seen from the air. Clouds, sunshine, trees and mountains would be important reference points. A fish would talk about experience in terms of water, coral, seaweed and other fish. Each has valid information, useful to a full understanding of the world, but each has a different perspective. If the bird told the fish something, the fish would have no way of knowing if it were true, and vice versa. To learn more about the world as a whole, each would have to accept the other's statements on faith, for each one speaks the truth from his unique perspective.

How do you broaden your perspective to include your customer's point of view? And how do you get him to listen to your ideas when his mental doors are closed? By validation and reciprocity.

JOAN: *"It sounds like what we discussed when we were dealing with Hedonistic Self and Altruistic Self [in Chapter 3]. Is there any real difference?"*

No difference in concept, only now we are dealing with perceptions of information rather than perceptions of self.

Say John tends to seek advice about things. His decision-making pattern is to seek external validation. Susan interprets other people's input regarding her decisions as interference. Her decision-making pattern is internal rather than external.

John and Susan interpret advice and information very differently. The issue is not what information you give, but how it is perceived. Both, however, will absorb new information to make a more informed decision if you communicate it the right way — a way they can accept — by first validating their knowledge, then giving them additional information from a different perspective.

DISTINGUISHING "OR" FROM "AND" IN COMMUNICATING POINTS OF VIEW

If you say, "A glass is half-empty," I can respond, "No, it's half-full." That rejects your point of view and implies that the cup must be either half-empty *or* half-full. However, if I say, "Yes, it's half-empty *and* it's half-full," I affirm your position and expand your point of view to include another perspective. By using "and" instead of "or," I am adding information rather than rejecting what you know to be true.

> RITA: *"But what if the person is truly wrong? What if he says, 'It's night' when it's day? What if he says, 'That purchase is a bad deal' when it's a good one?"*
>
> To you there is a clear answer, but for the buyer it is not so clear. The difference between the two is a function of information. Increased knowledge can bridge the gap.
>
> Say someone a blind person trusts tells him that it is

night. The blind person would believe him. If you said, "No, it is day," he wouldn't believe you. Wouldn't it be better to say, "I understand that you think it is night, and yet I see you in the sunlight — what do you think that means?" You are acknowledging his point of view and then adding additional information. Now, with these new facts, he can reevaluate his conclusions.

If a customer thinks the price on a property is poor, and you think it's good, you can say: "I'm sure you have good reason to believe the value isn't there, and yet the seller tells me he has three offers at his asking price. I wonder if it's true?" You have affirmed the customer and proposed another point of view. The customer can now process what you said and revise his conclusion without feeling rejected.

FOCUSING ON TEACHING AND LEARNING

To sell, you must both teach and learn. You will do this most successfully if you respect your customer's unique view of the world. That you don't agree with it is like a bird disagreeing with a fish — your differences are a result of each of you having a limited perspective. You must assume that what the buyer says is true, because *from his perspective it is*! If you learn what his position is and teach him yours, you will both gain understanding and, together, reach a more informed decision.

However, to teach and learn effectively, you must be in the right classroom.

JOHN: *"What do you mean by the 'right classroom'?"*
The classroom is a metaphor for the unique way a customer looks at, organizes and uses information. It is how he "sorts" new data and retrieves it for later use. To be rel-

evant to your customer and not seem like a nut reciting Shakespeare in a science class, you must communicate in a way that your customer can accept and understand so that he can effectively process it.

Once you identify how your customer most comfortably receives and organizes new information, you can present your data in that form so that it will be readily accepted and understood.

I am now going to define some common behavioral patterns that I have observed in customers.

⚘ PATTERN #1: AUTHORITY

This is the pattern I just described using John and Susan as examples. An *External Validator* wants advice when making a decision. An *Internal Validator* wants to be in complete control. The *Authority* spectrum looks like this:

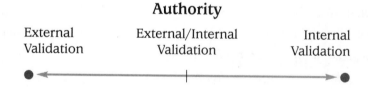

Authority

External Validation	External/Internal Validation	Internal Validation

When a buyer wants advice, you should validate this desire *and* give him an additional perspective by emphasizing his ability to rely on his own judgment. This new perspective is a form of information. It gives the customer a new way to evaluate the purchase.

An exercise will clarify what I mean. Debra, you be the apartment buyer who wants advice, and John, you be the broker. The asking price is $800,000.

JOHN: *"Hi, Debra, it's John from Bellmarc. I'm calling to get your thoughts on that home you saw with the asking price of $800,000."*

DEBRA: *"I'm not sure. I have to talk to my mother and brother about it. My brother is an investment banker and understands these things better than I do. They may want to see it."*

JOHN: *"Debra, I'm really pleased that you're thinking about having other people come to see the apartment. Obviously, you would do this only if you liked it, and I totally understand how getting additional input can clarify your thinking."*

DEBRA: *"Yes, it is a lot of money, and my family can help me make a wise decision."*

JOHN: *"I agree. They can help you on this. However, I am sure you also know that it is your home and that you alone will live there."*

DEBRA: *"Yes, I know that, but my family is important to me."*

JOHN: *"Of course! You should certainly get your family's assistance, and yet you will be sitting in the living room by yourself after everyone else is gone. Only you can decide if this home will make you happy."*

DEBRA: *"Yes, I guess that's true."*

JOHN: *"So you have two decisions to make. One involves other people and the other involves only you."*

DEBRA: *"Well, I guess so, but my family can help me."*

JOHN: *"Yes, they can, if you have first decided that you want this home. Why have them spend their time if you haven't thought about it for yourself first?"*

DEBRA: *"Well, I want it. That's why I want my family to see it."*

JOHN: *"And since you want it, they can confirm whether or not that is a wise decision."*

DEBRA: *"Yes, what they think is important."*

Okay, stop. Debra, what did you think?

DEBRA: *"I felt a little manipulated."*

That's because you were.

DEBRA: *"It didn't make me feel very good."*

When you sculpt, you manipulate the clay to form something beautiful. John was manipulating you to help you reach a conclusion that was richer and more empowering than one you could achieve on your own.

DEBRA: *"How so?"*

John did not tell you to ignore your family. In fact, he endorsed your desire to get their advice. However, he said their advice was not enough. *In addition,* you needed to make your own decision. He broadened your scope of thinking.

DEBRA: *"I felt that I was going somewhere I did not expect to go."*

You were, because your door to *Internal Validation* had been closed. John knocked on the door. And since he validated your desire for advice, you permitted him to show you another way as well.

Debra, did John push you to buy the property by saying you were wrong or insisting that you had to decide his way?

DEBRA: *"No, he just presented his view, and I thought about it."*

He didn't push you or disagree with you; he gave you additional information to help you make a better decision. Did John do anything improper?

DEBRA: *"I guess not."*

❧ PATTERN #2: MATCHING VS. MISMATCHING

In this pattern, the buyer either agrees or disagrees with whatever you say. A *Matcher* will agree with almost anything. If you say, "Wouldn't it be great to jump off the Brooklyn Bridge?" a Matcher will say, "Yes." If you say to a *Mismatcher*, "Isn't it a beautiful day?" he might reply, "It's too hot, and the sun is in my eyes."

This is a graphic presentation of this pattern:

Match vs. Mismatch

Match
(agreement)   Match/Mismatch   Mismatch
(disagreement)

Kids are great Mismatchers — it's part of their power play. If a parent says, "Eat your food!" you know the kid will say, "No!" If the parent says, "Don't eat your food," the kid eats!

I once put together a really great bank loan proposal. My attorney, who was experienced in dealing with this bank, told me he couldn't have done it better himself, as did a friend who worked for the bank.

When I met with a group of bank officers, however, the senior vice president in charge said: "I am not happy with this loan proposal. There are a lot of problems." Although dumbfounded, I answered: "Yes, you're right. I am not qualified for this loan, and the proposal is inadequate. I apologize for being inattentive to important things that are necessary to you." The senior vice president did a complete U-turn and said, "Okay, assuming we do the loan, what do you want?"

The senior vice president was a Mismatcher. When the document had nothing wrong, he said a lot was wrong. When I agreed with him and said the document was poor, he disagreed and said he would give me the loan. It's scary, but there are a lot of Mismatchers out there.

Let's try an exercise. Diane, you be a Mismatcher buyer, and Tina, you be the broker. The seller is asking $1,000,000 for the apartment.

TINA: *"Hi, Diane, it's Tina from Bellmarc. I'm calling to get your thoughts on that home we saw for $1,000,000. I thought it was really nice. What did you think?"*

DIANE: *"I thought it was horrible. It was too small, the building wasn't nice enough and it was too expensive."*

TINA: *"Yes. I thought the lobby was tacky, and I agree that the space was not as big as others you have seen. However, I'm sure you know that this is the only apartment for sale in the building in your price category."*

DIANE: *"That doesn't mean I should overpay. You should know that."*

TINA: *"That's true. You are not going to overpay just because it's the only apartment in the building. And yet, I remember you saying that you really like this building because it's convenient and has a garage and health club. I guess those things aren't really that important."*

DEBRA: *"Of course they're important! I am not going out into the rain and snow every time I want to exercise, and I hate parking my car and then having to trek home, especially when I have packages."*

TINA: *"Those things are really important, aren't they? However, you don't want this apartment, and it's not right for you, so we'll move on."*

DIANE: *"Well, let me think about it."*

Diane, you seemed to give in at the end of the conversation. What happened?

DIANE: *"I had no other choice. Even though I was trying to be adversarial with Tina, I was having difficulty avoiding the trap."*

The trap? Can't you call it seeing another point of view and reevaluating in light of this additional information?

DIANE: *"It wasn't just about seeing another viewpoint, it was about not being able to disagree. Even when I disagreed, I found myself agreeing with her."*

Is that because Tina's viewpoint had some merit? By validating your complaints and adding her own point of view, didn't Tina expand your knowledge? After all, she didn't pressure you to change your mind; she just got you to consider another perspective.

Tina used the same strategy as in the preceding exercise. First she validated you by affirming your complaints, and when she did so, you switched to the other side. Both reciprocity and your pattern of disagreement came into play. However, in the end all the information came out — your starting viewpoint and Tina's. The goal of increasing knowledge to enhance decision-making was achieved.

⌘ PATTERN #3: GENERAL VS. SPECIFIC

A *Generalist* uses words like "everyone" and "always." A *Specifier* dissects things into components and deals with them point by point. For example, a Specifier salesperson might describe an apartment by saying: "When you walk into the apartment, the kitchen is immediately to your left. The double stove is black, and the floor tiles are white. The ovens are on the left, etc., etc." A Generalist customer would be in anguish! Here's the spectrum of this pattern:

General vs. Specific

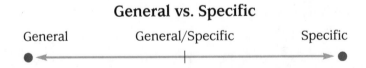

| General | General/Specific | Specific |

Salespeople get frustrated with Generalists because they aren't clear about their needs and objectives. A Generalist might state, "It doesn't feel right," which doesn't give enough information to resolve the problem. Or, if you ask what he wants, a Generalist might say, "I'll know it when I see it." And there is no easier way to annoy a Generalist than to demand specificity. You must phrase the request artfully, using validation and reciprocity.

> Let's do an exercise. David, you be a Generalist home buyer, and Gina, you be the broker. The house costs $1,000,000.

GINA: *"Hi, David, it's Gina from Bellmarc. Do you have a minute?"*

DAVID: *"Sure, Gina, what's up?"*

GINA: *"I'm calling about that house for $1,000,000. What did you think of it?"*

DAVID: *"I don't know, it just didn't feel right."*

GINA: *"I understand. It left you cold."*

DAVID: *"Something like that. I mean, it didn't have any charm."*

GINA: *"No charm. I see. It's important for a home to hit you right, and this home didn't do that for you. And yet, the price is extremely attractive, it has a lot of space and it's very sunny. I guess those things are important, too."*

DAVID: *"Yes. I mean, maybe. It was nice, I guess, but there was nothing special about it that sang out. It had no character."*

GINA: *"I see. You feel it lacks character. Character is important. However, if you put in your beautiful leather couch and bought a big mirror for the living room to emphasize the light and openness, and if you changed the kitchen cabinets and put in new appliances, it might start looking special."*

DAVID: *"Maybe, it's still is a little dreary, though."*

GINA: *"Yes, that's a problem. I, too, would be unhappy with something dreary. And yet, if you changed the wall colors and added window treatments and pictures, you could make it bright and cheerful. It might even sing."*

> Okay, let's stop. David, how did Gina do?

DAVID: *"At first, I thought Gina was condescending, but I found myself getting increasingly connected to what she was saying."*

So her first attempts to validate you and seek reciprocity were clumsy.

DAVID: *"Yes, but after the next round of conversation I started to get drawn in."*

You must try to be sincere in your validation and not just placate your buyer. Condescension is not an effective sales technique.

However, David may have also been undergoing a psychological shift. Customers frequently view salespeople as adversaries who will say anything to make a deal. By acknowledging the home's negatives, Gina contradicted that assumption. David would naturally wonder, "Why would Gina agree that this property is no good?" He would be confused, since his presumed adversary was acting as an ally. If she continued to affirm his beliefs and satisfy his ego, David would be compelled to recast Gina in a different role.

Gina, first you were General and then Specific. What was your strategy?

GINA: *"I listened to his general statement and affirmed it, then made as many specific suggestions as I could think of, one after the other."*

You listed specific interior decorating improvements that made the home more and more appealing with each item you added. This enriched David's information by infusing specifics.

David, were you aware that Gina was repeating your words and phrases back to you?

DAVID: *"I guess so, but I didn't notice because she added her own thoughts to mine. I felt like she understood my point."*

This is called *Backtracking*. You repeat a word or phrase used by the buyer. This adds validation and also creates a mental pause, which gives you time to process information and then formulate answers while appearing to maintain conversation.

Gina, you picked up on some of David's key words and phrases. When he said that nothing "sang out" about the home, you said you might be able to "make it sing." Echoing a buyer's key phrase makes him feel that you understand him and validate his position. When David said the house didn't "feel" right, you mirrored his sensory process by saying the house was "cold." Staying in a similar sensory form is also a powerful means of validating the customer.

🖎 PATTERN #4: PAST VS. FUTURE

In making a decision, one buyer might use past experience as his frame of reference while another might focus on the future and think in terms of potential rewards. In reality, both past experience and future expectations are valuable in making an informed decision. A great salesperson will help the customer expand his thinking to include both. The pattern spectrum looks like this:

Past vs. Future

Past	Past/Future	Future

Okay, Donna, you play a *Past-Oriented* home buyer with $1,000,000 to spend, and Sylvia, you play the broker.

SYLVIA: *"Donna? Hi, this is Sylvia from Bellmarc. Do you have a minute?"*

DONNA: *"Sure. Are you calling me about that apartment I saw?"*

SYLVIA: *"You got it. What do you think?"*

DONNA: *"I'm a little concerned. It doesn't have a third bedroom, and I've always had a third bedroom. Besides, I like old buildings, and this building is new. That bothers me."*

SYLVIA: *"I understand that you're used to having a third bedroom. Who wouldn't agree that a third bedroom is important? And old-world charm is special. New buildings just aren't built the way old ones were, I agree. And yet, think about the possibilities. Your children are grown, and you and your husband can make a fresh start. You are beginning a new adventure in which the two of you are free to do what you want. This is a new, fresh building for a new, fresh start."*

DONNA: *"I know, but my husband and I always had a third bedroom. What if the kids come to visit, or we need room for a study or something? It just wouldn't work for us."*

SYLVIA: *"I know the ways you're used to are comfortable, and that you want to be secure and confident in what you do. However, did you ever consider the advantages of living around young, dynamic people in a new building? You might find them a lot of fun to be around. Do you remember the fun you had when you were young, with young kids? I'm sure those were wonderful times, and you can live them again in another way."*

DONNA: *"I do remember those times fondly. I love to have kids around, it's true."*

SYLVIA: *"And now you have an opportunity to enjoy those old feelings in a new way. In fact, your grandchildren may want to visit you more because they will have kids there to play with."*

Okay, let's stop. Donna, what did you think about Sylvia's strategy?

DONNA: *"I thought it was great. She made me look at past experiences and future opportunities as effectively the same thing. I loved the idea of a fresh, new start to do old things in a new way. It hooked me right in. I also loved the idea that my grandchildren would probably want to see me more because there would be other kids around."*

Yes, Sylvia made you marry the past, present and future into one whole decision-making process. This expanded your thinking and enriched your decision.

✐ PATTERN #5: PROBLEM VS. OPPORTUNITY

Do you know people who always dwell on problems? They are *Problem Avoiders*. Whereas *Opportunity Seekers* say, "There are no problems, just challenges that present opportunities." They see every event as a chance to profit. Opportunity Seekers say things like, "Give me a chance" or "I think we can do this." They have an empowering perspective. Problem Avoiders like to be secure.

Here's the pattern spectrum:

Problem vs. Opportunity

Problem	Problem/Opportunity	Opportunity

Let's do an exercise. David, you play a *Problem-Avoiding* home buyer with $1,000,000 to spend, and Diane, you play the broker.

DIANE: *"Hi, David, this is Diane from Bellmarc. Do you have a minute?"*

DAVID: *"Sure, Diane, what can I do for you?"*

DIANE: *"I'm calling about that apartment we saw. You know, the one for $1,000,000. What did you think of it?"*

DAVID: *"I think there are a lot of problems. The apartment needs* *a lot of work, and the price is too high. There is one problem after another."*

DIANE: *"No question about it, these are real problems. Construction costs are enormous, and apartments are priced sky-high. However, David, does the location work for you?"*

DAVID: *"Yes."*

DIANE: *"How about the building?"*

DAVID: *"The building is fine."*

DIANE: *"Is the apartment big enough, and do you like the views?"*

DAVID: *"Sure."*

DIANE: *"You know, there are problems here. No question. However, there is also an opportunity because it has the location and aesthetic qualities you want. If we can get it at a fair price, maybe this could be the one."*

DAVID: *"But what about the construction? That's an enormous headache."*

DIANE: *"You're right, that's a problem with this apartment. And yet, when you finish the construction, you will have exactly what you want. A lot of people prefer constructing their homes because they can make them just the way they want them. This could be your chance to do that."*

DAVID: *"But it's too expensive."*

DIANE: *"Yes, that's a problem. However, it's just an asking price. Let's put in a lower offer — we might get a good counteroffer."*

Okay, let's stop. David, how was Diane's performance?

DAVID: *"Whenever I said something was a problem, Diane minimized it and focused on the good features. She made me look at it another way."*

She did. She *reframed* your problems; she restated them as opportunities. It is an important characteristic of a good salesperson. She affirmed that each problem existed and that it was real, then showed you how to make the problem go away or become an opportunity. I liked the way she dissected your definition of a good apartment. She made you acknowledge the ways in which the apartment worked for you and that the only real issue was getting a good price. Then she overcame your resistance by encouraging you to take a shot.

This pattern is particularly tricky because you must marry a somber, hesitant outlook to one that is ambitious and euphoric. When Problem Avoiders are shown the opportunity in a situation, they often become uncomfortable. They don't cope easily with a positive outlook.

Getting a Problem Avoider to any kind of hybrid view requires you to express a broad level of empathy. You can propose the opportunity inherent in the situation only after sincerely affirming his fears and building trust. You may not agree with his issues, but you should agree that he has a right to think differently than you do.

✿ PATTERN #6: RANDOM VS. SEQUENTIAL

Random Thinkers can't stick to a topic. One moment they're discussing the purchase, and the next they're talking about going to a department store. There are no boundaries to the conversation. Conversations with *Sequential Thinkers* proceed logically; Random Thinkers take forever to get to the point.

The pattern spectrum looks like this:

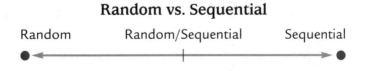

Random vs. Sequential

| Random | Random/Sequential | Sequential |

John, you play the Random buyer, and Rita, you play the broker. Let's keep the price at $1,000,000.

RITA: *"Hi, John, this is Rita from Bellmarc. What do you think of that apartment we saw for $1,000,000?"*

JOHN: *"It was lovely. By the way, I'm going to Lutèce tonight — have you ever eaten there?"*

RITA: *"It's a wonderful restaurant. I love French food. Have you ever been to France? I love Paris."*

JOHN [Turning to Neil]: *"Hey, this is ridiculous."*

I agree. Rita, when validating a Random Thinker, be careful not to stray down random pathways. Validate the random statement, then lead the conversation back to the point. Be artful, but keep your eye on the ball.

RITA: *"Okay."*

Good, let's start again.

RITA: *"Hi, this is Rita from Bellmarc. John, I'm calling to see if you liked the apartment I showed you for $1,000,000."*

JOHN: *"Yes, it was lovely. I did like it. Hey, did you ever go to Lutèce? I'm going there tonight."*

RITA: *"You are? I've never been there, but I've heard it's terrific, and I know you'll have a good time. By the way, the seller of that apartment is hoping to hear from me; what should I say?"*

JOHN: *"It was really nice. I liked it. I hope I can get out of work on time tonight so I won't have to rush."*

RITA: *"I won't bother you if you're in a rush. I know you have a lot on your mind. But should I tell the apartment owner that you liked it?"*

JOHN: *"I did like it, but I'm not sure. There are still a lot of apartments I haven't seen. I need to get this report out. Oh, God."*

RITA: *"Look, you work on that report. I can see that you're busy, so I'll tell you what I recommend. First, let's put in a low offer of $900,000. Second, I will line up some other apartments for you* *to look at so you will have more choices. Third, we will talk to-morrow after I hear from the seller. And fourth, you can tell me about the restaurant. What do you think?"*

Okay, let's stop. John, did Rita's sequential strategy work?

JOHN: *"I really liked it. It was like I was wandering around, and someone finally put me on track."*

How did you feel when Rita included making an offer in the sequence of steps?

JOHN: *"I was receptive to it as long as I was seeing other apartments. I didn't feel committed; it was just one item on the list. I especially liked it when Rita segued into the restaurant. It was additional validation, and it kept me in."*

In dealing with a Random Thinker, you have to spend time on topics he selects and not get disoriented as he veers off on random byways. Once you have his rhythm of conversation properly paced, you can keep leading him back to the sequential alternative. You have to keep getting him back on track in a subtle, artful way.

SYLVIA: *"I loved the way Rita used the words 'By the way' to get John back on track. It was like she was discussing the restaurant as the primary issue and the apartment was a side issue. I felt that she was validating John's randomness, not just his topic."*

Yes, I liked that too. John felt comfortable because it conformed to his pattern.

SYLVIA: *"I guess a Random Thinker is difficult to deal with?"*

Hardly. We all stray from the point now and then. Most of us free-associate in some conversations and follow logical, sequential patterns in others. Random Thinkers are not hard to work with unless you demand that they address your concerns without your first validating their chosen topics. They understand the nature of sequential thinking

even if they don't conform to it. You will get where you
want to go — you just can't let yourself become disoriented or distracted from your goal along the way.

⚘ BEHAVIORAL PATTERNS IN PRACTICE

The key to rapport with your customer is validation of self and conform-
ity to your customer's program for analyzing information.

How do you think that understanding behavioral patterns
will help you sell?

SYLVIA: *"It gives me a new way to think about the customer. Each
pattern is a kind of theme. If I can get the customer's theme
right, I can connect with him."*

Yes. These patterns are a powerful means of connecting
with your buyer and his decision-making process.

RITA: *"I'm still bothered that I felt manipulated. I didn't end the
conversation feeling excited; I felt cautious, as if the salesperson
was trying to get me to do something I would rather not do."*

When you ask a customer to think in a way that is incon-
sistent with his typical process, he may realize the value of
your information yet still feel uncomfortable. You must be
sensitive to this and be respectful. Your validation, if sincere, should overcome his reservations. His desire to reciprocate will help you connect with him and lead to a relationship of trust.

RON: *"Are the patterns you identified the only ones that exist, or
are there others?"*

No, these are just the most common patterns. Any theme
that occurs repeatedly in the course of conversation can
clue you in to the customer's decision-making process. You

can then see what information is being ignored and try to introduce it in a nonthreatening way after validating the customer's perceived concerns. It can help to imagine the conversation with the customer before it happens. You can experiment with different approaches before actually having the conversation.

❧ SUMMARY

Good communication involves acknowledging that each individual has a unique perspective. Even if they don't make sense to you, your buyer's reservations are very real from his point of view. You must acknowledge the buyer's reservations and validate his viewpoint before you can expect him to listen to yours.

Many people, however, share common patterns in decision-making. If you validate the customer's pattern, this will make him feel acknowledged and respected, and he will reciprocate by listening to your point of view. You can then enhance the decision-making process by introducing information that the customer is missing. Recognizing the pattern is the first step in this process.

JOAN: *"What is the 'or vs. and' principle?"*
When you say, "The glass is half-full or half-empty," you imply that it must be one or the other — it can't be both. Words like "or" or "but" make you choose between two competing sets of information. Words like "and," "and yet" and "also" acknowledge the customer's legitimate position and permit you to add information since there has been no rejection.

DONNA: *"Why must a salesperson be both a teacher and a student?"*

You must *learn* about your customer's needs and teach him the merits of various alternatives.

SYLVIA: *"What is Backtracking?"*

Repeating a statement made by the customer as the lead-in to your reply. Backtracking is very validating. It also creates a mental pause, extending your time to develop an answer while maintaining a seamless conversation.

ROBERT: *"What are the most common behavioral patterns?"*

#1 AUTHORITY. Some customers seek advice; they are External Validators. Others make decisions independently; they are Internal Validators.

#2 MATCHING VS. MISMATCHING. Some customers either agree or disagree with anything you say.

#3 GENERAL VS. SPECIFIC. Some customers speak in generalities; others are specific about their needs.

#4 PAST VS. FUTURE. Some customers stick with what has worked in the past and play it safe; others focus on future possibilities and potential rewards.

#5 PROBLEM VS. OPPORTUNITY. Some customers focus on problems; others focus on opportunities.

#6 RANDOM VS. SEQUENTIAL. Some customers can't stick to the subject; others are logical and think in terms of sequences or steps.

๏

Failure Is the Key to Success

ONCE A MAN SOUGHT ABSOLUTE KNOWLEDGE. IN THIS PURSUIT, HE JOURNEYED TO INDIA, WHERE HE HAD HEARD THAT A VERY WISE MAN LIVED HIGH IN THE HIMALAYAN MOUNTAINS.

AFTER GREAT EFFORT, HE REACHED HIS DESTINATION AND ENTERED THE CAVE WHERE THE WISE MAN LIVED. THERE, THE TRAVELER SAW A DIRTY AND UNSHAVEN MAN SITTING NEAR A FIRE. HIS EYES WERE CLOSED, AND HE SAT IN THE LOTUS POSITION OF DEEP MEDITATION. THE TRAVELER SAID: "OH, WISE ONE, I HAVE CROSSED GREAT SEAS FOR YOUR WISDOM. GUIDE ME WITH YOUR TRUTHS!"

THE WISE MAN OPENED HIS EYES AND SAID: "TELL ME OF THE PLACE YOU WERE BORN. TELL ME ABOUT YOUR HOME AND THE THINGS YOU HAVE DONE." THE TRAVELER THEN SPOKE OF HIS HOME, HIS JOB AND HIS READINGS. HE SPOKE ABOUT THE JOURNEY HE HAD TAKEN TO COME TO THIS PLACE, THE PEOPLE HE HAD MET AND THE LESSONS HE HAD LEARNED ON THE WAY. HE SPOKE OF THE HAPPINESS HE HAD SEEN AND THE MISERY.

AFTER THIS LONG STORY WAS TOLD, THE WISE MAN SAID: "WHEN I WAS A BOY, I ATE A PEAR. IT WAS ROTTEN, AND I SPIT IT OUT. IT FELL ON THE GROUND AND WAS EATEN BY FLIES. I SAID TO MYSELF, 'NOW I KNOW THE TASTE OF A BAD PEAR AND HAVE LEARNED SOMETHING I WILL NEVER FORGET,' AND I LOOKED AT THE FLIES AND SAID: 'THE PEAR DID NOT GO TO WASTE. THAT IS GOOD.'"

THE TRAVELER, FRUSTRATED, SAID: "WHAT ARE THESE RIDDLES? WHY DON'T YOU SHARE YOUR WISDOM WITH ME?" THE WISE MAN ANSWERED: "I CANNOT. I DON'T HAVE ANY ANSWERS. I CAME HERE TO ESCAPE MY FAILURES, TO ABANDON

REAL PEOPLE AND A REAL WORLD THAT I COULD NOT LIVE IN."

THE TRAVELER WAS DUMBFOUNDED. "SURELY THERE IS MORE TO YOUR LIFE THAN THAT," HE SAID. "EVERYONE I MET HAS TOLD ME OF YOUR WISDOM. SOME EVEN SAID YOU GAVE THEM THE SECRET TO THEIR SUCCESS." THE WISE MAN REPLIED: "YES, I AM AN EXAMPLE OF WHAT CAN HAPPEN WHEN YOU ARE AFRAID OF YOURSELF AND THE WORLD AROUND YOU. I AM THE ULTIMATE FAILURE. MY WISDOM IS NOT IN MY KNOWLEDGE, BUT IN MY MESSAGE."

THE TRAVELER WAS CONFUSED. HE ASKED: "WHY DO YOU STAY HERE?" THE WISE ONE ANSWERED. "BECAUSE IN MY FAILURE I HAVE FOUND MY GREATEST SUCCESS!"

THE TRAVELER BEGAN TO REALIZE THE ULTIMATE TRUTH THAT EACH EVENT'S MEANING DEPENDED ON THE JUDGE — THAT GOODNESS, HAPPINESS, SADNESS AND EVIL WERE ALL POINTS OF VIEW THAT EXISTED TOGETHER. IT WAS THE TASK OF EACH OBSERVER TO CHOOSE WHICH TO SEE.

THE TRAVELER THEN WALKED DOWN THE MOUNTAIN AND WENT BACK TO HIS HOME AND LIVED WITH GREAT HAPPINESS AND SUCCESS EVER AFTER.

CHAPTER 5

❧

Communicating with a Bio-Computer

A computer responds to given inputs with predictable out-puts. So do people. Your customer's outputs are his re-sponses. If you understand how to read responses, both verbal and nonverbal, you will learn which methods of presenting information will be most the effective for him.

❧ BEING A BIO-COMPUTER

There are many ways in which humans are like computers. When you enter data into a computer, it runs the way it was programmed. It also stores information. To retrieve information, it first accesses electronic memory, then goes to a secondary memory storage system commonly found on a hard disk. Electronic memory is more readily accessible than the hard disk, but its storage capacity is limited.

When you need an answer from a computer, you first input data. That data is processed in electronic memory, then the computer retrieves additional data from the hard disk to complete the processing before forming a conclusion. In diagram form it looks like this:

Inputs → Processing → Retrieval → Processing → Outputs

Our minds work the same way. Data comes in, we think about it, we access our memories, we think about it some more, then we formulate our conclusions (outputs).

Let's do a test. John, I'm handing you an object, what is it?

JOHN: *"A pen."*

You said that pretty fast. Did you have to think about it?

JOHN: *"Of course not — it's a pen."*

When did you last write a letter with a pen?

JOHN: *"Well...I wrote to my parents when I vacationed in Switzerland. I really don't write letters much."*

Why did you pause before you answered?

JOHN: *"Because I had to think about it. I had to remember when I last wrote a letter."*

And that took extra effort?

JOHN: *"Yes."*

Yet once you remembered when you wrote the letter, you recalled where as well?

JOHN: *"Yes, I can see the hotel room where I wrote it."*

Did I ask for that information?

JOHN: *"No, it was part of remembering when I wrote the letter. I saw a picture of myself writing it, then answered your question by looking at the picture."*

John answered the first question, about the pen, immediately, so that was the equivalent of electronic memory. He had to think about the next question. First he processed that he needed additional information. Then he retrieved that information from his "hard disk" of memories, processed it to pick out what was relevant and, finally, answered the question. He acted like a computer.

John also accessed his memory as a picture. This is useful information.

❧ SENSORY STRATEGIES

You emphasize one of your three primary senses (sight, hearing or feeling) over the others. This is your *lead sensory system*. John answered my question by calling up a picture — his lead system is visual.

> [Neil hands the pen to Susan.]
> Susan, tell me what you are thinking about the pen.
> **SUSAN:** *"I'm not sure what you mean, but when I write a letter it's because I miss someone and want to stay in contact."*
> Is there a picture?
> **SUSAN:** *"No, I just feel an urge to write. I'm sad that someone is away and want to say that I miss him and care about him."*
> Can anyone tell me what Susan's lead sensory system is?
> **BETH:** *"Feeling. My own feelings were stimulated by the words she used."*

Yes, John used words like "look," "see" and "picture," while Susan used words like "feel," "miss" and "urge." These sensory words are called *predicates* and provide an important clue to the sensory form a person is thinking in.

Another important cue is eye movements. Most people look up as they access visual memories and look down as they access feelings.

Let's do an experiment. I want each of you to look up and picture a special moment from your last vacation. While the picture is vivid in your mind, look down. Try to keep the picture clear.

> **JOHN:** *"I couldn't do it. When I looked down the picture disappeared."*
> Here's why: Your brain stores data from your different senses in distinct areas, and your eyes reflect the process of retrieval. When you look up, you are accessing your visual

memories. When you look down, you are accessing memories stored as feelings. By looking down, you disconnected from the visual storage area.

RITA: *"Are there cues for other senses as well?"*

Try this. Each of you look at the person next to you. One of you be the subject, the other be the observer. Each subject should remember a tune he liked when he was younger.

Okay, let's discuss the results. Steve?

STEVE: *"Sara's eyes moved to the right."*

RITA: *"I saw the same thing with Beth."*

SUSAN: *"John's eyes first moved up, then sideways."*

John, did you picture a performer playing the song before you remembered the tune?

JOHN: *"Yes."*

So you took a series of steps, and your eye movements reflected your process.

JOHN: *"Yes, getting a picture of what I am thinking about clears things up for me."*

I see your point. Focusing on the image adds clarity to your picture and brightens things up. Afterward, you can tune right in. [Everyone laughs.]

I'm glad you got what I was doing. By matching John's visual processing with visual predicates, I was validating his process. I added an auditory predicate at the end to validate the second step of his process. What if I had done the auditory first?

RITA: *"Since John's lead sensory system is visual, he wouldn't feel as connected, either to you or to what you were saying."*

Right. If I used auditory predicates first, there would be no connection between my words and the way he processed information.

JOHN: *"Does everyone have a lead sensory system for processing information?"*

Absolutely, and if you can identify this lead sensory system, you can match it with your words to create rich rapport. The more aware you are of your buyer's sensory processing strategy, the more you can use matching predicates and the more powerful your connection will be.

SYLVIA: *"Don't you want to first validate the customer's lead sensory process and then introduce him to information from the other senses?"*

There's a big difference between providing new information and using effective words to make your argument. Earlier, we explored giving the customer more information to offer a broader range of choices. By identifying the buyer's processing strategy, however, you are figuring out how to word your argument so it will get through. You want to choose words that feel right, look right or sound right.

JOHN: *"Are there other ways to use words or gestures to create rapport?"*

Many communication habits can be effectively validated. I know someone who nods his head when someone else is speaking, and I always nod my head when I listen to him. Another person I know plays with his pen while he talks. When speaking to him, I grasp my hands and fidget with my fingers. This subconsciously validates his habit of fidgeting and builds rapport.

People who point and step forward as they talk are visual thinkers. It is as if they are saying, "See my point?" People who show the palms of their hands or bend slightly at the knees are expressing a kinesthetic (feeling) process. They are saying, "I'm begging you to feel my experience."

> People who cross their legs, clasp their hands in their laps
> and sit with their backs straight are processing auditorial-
> ly. They're saying, "I am tuned in to what you are saying."

It is useful to match your buyers' body language and their sensory
words to enrich your connection. However, mirroring their mannerisms
or conforming your body language to their sensory patterns must be
done subtly and with sincerity.

For example: A buyer enters an apartment and immediately sits
down. He strokes the furniture and then gets up to look at the view. At
the next apartment, he again touches the furniture, then inspects the
view. Seeing this, the salesperson touches the sofa and says: "Gee, these
couches are great. Aren't the pillows comfortable?" Then he looks out
the window and says: "I wouldn't mind sitting on this couch for a while
and looking at this view. That would feel great at the end of a long day."
The salesperson identified the customer's strategy of processing information first kinesthetically and then visually. He used the same strategy in his communication, thereby validating the buyer and building rapport. The buyer will subconsciously recognize that the salesperson
shares his perspective and understands his underlying motivation for
making a decision.

JOHN: *"Is it easy to identify a customer's strategy?"*
It depends on the customer. Some immediately move their
eyes up and use lots of visual predicates. They clearly
process information visually. Others have more complex
strategies. I look for the lead process and observe the customer's response to my words and actions to test my
hypothesis. The ultimate test is whether what I do is effective in creating the right connection between us.
BETH: *"You discussed visual, kinesthetic and auditory sensory
cues but didn't mention smell or taste. Aren't they important?"*

Smell and taste are rarely sensory leads. People get the bulk of their experience through sight, feelings and sounds.

❧ UNDERSTANDING NONVERBAL COMMUNICATION

Communication is not just what you say, but how you say it. A major university study found that 95% of all communication is nonverbal. Only 5% of your meaning is expressed by the words you use!

Think about my meaning as I say the word "no."

"Hmmm, no." [Neil starts on a high tone, then lowers it. His body tilts to one side, and his arms are folded.]

"No!" [Neil stands forward. He points his finger and stares straight ahead. His tone is sharp and strong.]

"No?" [Neil sits, his head turned to one side. The palms of his hands are up and forward, and he moves his body forward as he speaks. His voice starts low, then gets higher.]

"No." [Neil sits, his head slightly turned. He moves his upper body forward, his eyebrows furrowed. His tone is high with a slight inflection. His arms are folded in front of him.]

All I said was "no." Isn't that correct?

DAVID: *"Yes, but you meant very different things."*

Yes, my voice, posture and facial expressions, not just my words, helped to convey my meaning. Understanding these variations is important in interpreting your customer's meaning.

Let's do an exercise in which each of you evaluates what someone is saying without his saying a word. Look for physical changes as he processes different thoughts. Observe the type and degree of change as well as the final form the thought takes in his face and posture.

As you do this exercise, think about the difference between judgments and observations. A judgment is the meaning you give to something. An observation is neutral. For example, to say someone looked happy is a judgment. What you saw was an upward curve of the lips. Your interpretation of this as a smile and your conclusion that the person was happy is a judgment. In this exercise I want only observations, not judgments.

I will demonstrate with Brad, then we will split into groups. Watch Brad. Look for physical changes.

> Brad, think of someone you like. Make the picture clear in your mind. [A minute passes.]
>
> Now erase that picture and make your mind blank.
>
> Now I want you to think of someone you do not like. Again, make this picture as clear as you can. [A minute passes.]

> David, what did you see when Brad thought about someone he liked?

DAVID: *"Brad's lips raised at the ends and he sank a little in his seat and looked up. He folded his arms in front of him, and his breathing deepened."*

> What about when Brad thought about someone he did not like?

DAVID: *"He sat up straighter, and his lips were pursed. He put his hands on the arms of his chair, lowered his eyes and blinked more often. His face went a little flaccid, and his head turned slightly down."*

> Thank you, David. These are very good observations.

Now everyone pair up and do this exercise, and we will discuss your findings.

[The class performs the exercise.]

Did anyone have trouble identifying changes in his or her partner?

BARBARA: *"John always seemed to have the same expression. I didn't see any change. His eyebrows went up for someone he liked, and his eyes went down for someone he didn't like, but he kept the same neutral expression."*

You're interpreting his neutral expression as meaning he didn't change. However, his eyes and eyebrows changed. Any identifiable change is enough. Let's say his eyebrows always go up when he thinks of things he likes, and his eyes always go down when he thinks of things he doesn't like. What if he said he didn't like an apartment you showed him, but his eyebrows went up?

BARBARA: *"I might think he really liked it. If his eyes and words were contradictory, I would want to explore further."*

All you need is a sign — a clue to what the customer is really thinking. You don't need a blaring trumpet. A squeak will do, even a little squeak. Even a subtle change can signal that something is going on.

Don't assume that a smile means the buyer is happy. It might be politeness, inattention or something else. You may smile only when you are happy, but your buyer may not — observe and find out.

When you meet a customer, ask what qualities in a product would make him happy. Listen carefully to the words, but remember that words are only 5% of the communication. Watch his face as he describes his ideal product. Observe his body position, his breathing, his movements and what he does with his hands. Focus on his eyes and expressions. Listen to the tone of his voice. Look for changes. These are the physical cues that will alert you to when your customer is happy.

Then ask your customer to tell you what he dislikes in a product. Focus on the changes in his voice, body movements and expressions from when he was happy. These cues will alert you to when the customer is unhappy.

A real estate broker showing an apartment with a terrible kitchen might ask the buyer, "So, what do you think of this kitchen?" The buyer's body movements, eyes, breathing and expressions will tell the observant broker what the customer's cues are when he doesn't like something. Then, if the view is spectacular, the broker could ask, "So, what do you think of this view?" and observe the buyer's physical changes.

Once you find your customer's cues, you will know how he feels without a lot of interference. Notice his voice's tone and tempo, facial changes and body movements — these don't lie.

Most customers won't tell you what they are really thinking; they don't want to have to defend themselves. However, you can normally tell what they are saying without words. Leave your judgments behind and observe the facts for what they are — then use those facts to find solutions.

JANE: *"What if you can't find physical cues to a person's likes and dislikes?"*

Then you have to rely on his words and keep observing as closely as you can. First focus on determining his lead sensory processing strategy (visual, kinesthetic or auditory) and use matching sensory words to build rapport. As the customer becomes more comfortable with you, he may start to reveal more physical variations.

冂Ӥ۹ SUMMARY

This chapter explores nonverbal communication. It teaches that each customer emphasizes one of his three primary senses (sight, hearing or feeling) in processing information and reaching conclusions. It teaches how to find your customer's lead sensory system and match it with your language to create strong rapport. It also shows you how to become alert to nonverbal, physical cues that will reveal your customer's true feelings.

> **RENE:** *"How are people bio-computers?"*
>
> We each have predictable patterns of behavior. As with a computer, if a user understands how the program works, he can access the system. If you figure out your buyer's behavior and thought patterns, you can communicate more effectively.
>
> **JOAN:** *"What is a buyer's* sensory strategy?"
>
> We each process new ideas and experiences using our visual, auditory or feeling (kinesthetic) senses in a habitual sequence. If you understand the customer's sensory lead and subsequent patterns, you can match them with your language to build rapport and persuade.
>
> **DONNA:** *"What are* predicates, *and how are they important?"*
>
> Predicates are words that refer to sight, sound or feeling. The customer's use of predicates can indicate how he processes information. If you can identify the customer's lead sensory process, you can use similar predicates in your speech, thereby validating the customer's process and forging a strong connection with him.
>
> **JONATHAN:** *"What does it mean if the customer looks up to remember something?"*
>
> He is accessing memories that are visual. This is a cue that

you should speak to him with words that are consistent with this lead process.

SYLVIA: *"What if he looks down?"*

He is accessing memories through his feelings. This is a cue that you should speak to him in words that are consistent with this kinesthetic process.

RITA: *"How much of communication is verbal?"*

Only 5%; 95% is voice intonation and tempo, facial expression, body position and movement and other physical indicators.

JONATHAN: *"How do you read a customer's physical indicators?"*

You observe his physical changes when he responds to things he likes and things he doesn't like. Don't make judgments or assumptions — observe the buyer's movements and expressions carefully and objectively until his patterns become clear. His body won't lie, even when his words do.

❧

Nice in the Right Way

A SALESPERSON WAS NOT MAKING DEALS. WHILE SPEAKING TO HER, I FOUND MYSELF LIKING HER MORE AND MORE, AND I STARTED TO REALIZE THE NATURE OF HER PROBLEM.

I ASKED, "ARE YOU NICE LIKE THIS TO ALL YOUR CUSTOMERS?" SHE ANSWERED, "WHY, OF COURSE, ALL MY CUSTOMERS SAY THEY REALLY LIKE ME." I RESPONDED: "YES, YOU'RE SO NICE THAT ALL I'M THINKING ABOUT IS HOW NICE YOU ARE. THE KEY IS TO BE NICE IN A FOCUSED WAY SO THAT YOU BUILD RAPPORT TO SELL AND MAKE MONEY."

THE PROBLEM AFFLICTING THIS SALESPERSON WAS THAT SHE NEVER THOUGHT ABOUT BEING NICE; IT JUST SORT OF HAPPENED. SHE BLAMED HER PARENTS FOR HER NICENESS, SAYING, "THAT'S JUST THE WAY I WAS BROUGHT UP."

I ADVISED HER THAT THE NEXT TIME SHE MET A CUSTOMER, SHE SHOULD MAKE A MENTAL PICTURE OF HERSELF WITH THAT CUSTOMER, THEN MAKE HERSELF BIGGER AND THE CUSTOMER SMALLER. "NOW GO INTO YOURSELF, POINT AT THE CUSTOMER AND SAY, 'I EAT YOU FOR BREAKFAST — YOU'RE MY NEXT SALE!'"

SHE WAS SHOCKED BY MY LANGUAGE AND THOUGHT I WAS KIDDING. I WAS NOT.

I ASKED HER WHAT WOULD HAPPEN IF SHE DID AS I SUGGESTED. SHE PONDERED A BIT AND REALIZED THAT BY DOING WHAT I ASKED SHE WAS EMPOWERING HERSELF. SHE NO LONGER THOUGHT ABOUT BEING NICE TO BE VALIDATED; SHE WAS BEING NICE FOR A REASON AND COULD GAIN GREATER CONTROL OVER THE OUTCOME OF THE CONVERSATION.

❧

CHAPTER 6

Picturing the Sale from the Right Perspective

If you can envision the sale from the customer's perspective, you will be able to enrich his picture and excite him about making a purchase.

ENRICHING AWARENESS

Your awareness encompasses every experience you have ever had, both real and imaginary. This wisdom is always there for you to explore and discover new feelings and new meanings.

Create a picture in your mind. See yourself on a beach on a beautiful sunny day. The sun is warm and comforting. The sand is white, and the water is turquoise blue. Along the beach, palm trees sway back and forth in the wind. The sand on the beach is soft and feels like satin against your skin. The cool, clear water rushes forward with a whooshing sound, then loses energy and recedes...forward and then back. Feel the calmness and the warmth. Picture the white sand and blue sea, the green leaves rustling back and forth in the breeze.

Notice how you feel. Be aware of the pictures and sounds.

Make the picture bigger and clearer and increase the sound.

Now put a frame around the picture. Make it smaller and dimmer. Decrease the level of sound. [Neil pauses.]

Good, now everyone come down to earth and let's talk about it. John, what did you think about this exercise?

JOHN: *"I got caught up in the picture. I was there."*

Truly, you were. To the mind, there is no such thing as pretend. Your mind responds as if the picture were reality, especially when your primary senses of sight, hearing and feeling are integrated into the process. Did anyone notice how I did this?

SARA: *"Yes, you used different predicates: visual, auditory and feeling (kinesthetic)."*

Yes. Predicates, words that stimulate a sensory response, are a powerful way to enrich the picture. I identified colors to enhance the visual experience, created kinesthetic sensations with words like soft and warm, and called up auditory sensations with "whooshing" and "rustling." Did anyone notice anything else?

SARA: *"You used words and phrases like 'back and forth' and 'forward' and 'recedes.'"*

Yes, the mind works in terms of spectrums. By having the picture include the full range of choices, I invited inclusion of all possible thoughts.

SARA: *"I felt like I was in a trance."*

You were. A trance is a fixation on a specific thought or process. When your mind centered on the picture, it became real enough that your body responded biochemically. When you altered the context of the picture, not the content, did that biochemical response change?

SARA: *"The first set of changes, making the picture bigger and so on, gave me more intense feelings. With the second set of alterations, the feelings became less intense."*

These qualities of context are called *submodalities*, and they can powerfully enrich or minimize an experience.

∾ CONNECTING TO THE CUSTOMER'S PERSPECTIVE

How would you talk to a customer about your product after he has seen it? How could you use submodalities to enhance it for the buyer?

> Say your product is a two-bedroom apartment with solid, smooth white walls. It has a wonderful city view — a kaleidoscope of lights that shimmer at night like an array of tiny stars. The kitchen countertop is hard marble, and the cabinets are a warm tan color with brass handles.

JOHN: *"I am getting feelings about it as you describe it with sensory words."*

Yes, and you are becoming connected to the experience.

SARA: *"But I can't see myself creating a picture for the customer as you have done, and I'm not going to tell him to make it bigger and brighter."*

> Good point. But can you create a picture of your customer in your mind?

SARA: *"Sure."*

What is the customer wearing?

SARA: *"He has on a gray suit."*

> Notice the details including the background and whether your customer is sitting or standing. Make the picture rich and clear.
>
> Now make a second picture, one of yourself. Make this clearer and richer as well.
>
> Now you have two pictures in your mind — one of your customer and one of yourself.
>
> Next see yourself walking away from the place where you were located and going into the customer's body. You are inside of him, and he is a costume that you are wearing.
>
> Now become the customer. Feel the flow of sensations

through his body. Be aware of his thoughts. Notice what is important to him — and how you have become him.

At this point, look at the apartment from his perspective. Find visual qualities that appeal to you, kinesthetic qualities that stimulate your feelings and notice the sounds.

Once you have seen, felt and heard this apartment in the body of your customer, I want you to make the picture bigger, brighter, clearer and three-dimensional.

As the customer, you have become aware of this apartment with all of your senses. You have seen features that you respond to and features that turn you off. Both are there: the good and bad, the important and unimportant. With your new awareness, can you judge the apartment as something you should consider or not?

SARA: *"Yes."*

What if you did this exercise before you showed the customer an apartment? Would you show it the same way?

SARA: *"No, I have become more committed to the apartment as something I want to talk about, and I am more sensitive to my customer's preferences."*

All you did was pretend, but in your mind you became the customer, you understood better how he thinks and feels. When you meet in the apartment, you will connect with him in an expanded way and be able to give him a richer picture, using words consistent with his sensory-processing strategy.

SARA: *"I would definitely be more enthusiastic in showing the apartment, and I think I would communicate more effectively with the customer."*

You can do this to sell any product, service or idea. The key is to step into the customer. Focus on the visual, auditory and kinesthetic qualities the customer will respond to. See the product as he will see it. Then you can sell the product on the customer's terms. Remember, the decision whether or not to buy is his, not yours.

DIMINISHING INTENSITY

Let's now explore the effect of minimizing the experience and its impact on your feelings.

What happened when you put a frame around the picture and made it smaller and darker?

SARA: *"The intensity was diminished."*

Yes. Can you see how that would be useful?

Try this: Picture an argument in which someone said something that hurt or offended you. Concentrate on yourself and the person who hurt you. See what you are both wearing and the other person's expression as he talks to you.

Make the picture bigger, brighter, clearer and three-dimensional.

Then place the picture on a movie screen. As you watch the argument on the screen, notice that you are sitting alone in the theater. It's just you looking at the screen watching the argument.

Now see yourself in the projection booth. As you look down, see yourself sitting in the movie theater and on the screen. You are having the argument, but you are also watching from a seat in the theater and from the projection booth. [Neil pauses.]

Sara, what happened?

SARA: *"I don't like to think about the past, particularly if it is painful. When you asked me to make the picture bigger and brighter, it made me only more uncomfortable. However, when I put the picture on the screen, my feelings subsided, and when I was watching from the movie theater, I felt even more removed. Finally, when I went to the projection booth, I left my feelings behind. I was looking at the scene neutrally."*

And as you looked at it neutrally, you could consider it rationally. The emotions were left on the screen so you could analyze the alternatives and find the best way to deal with the situation.

SARA: *"The argument became less important, removed and under control."*

Yes, and if you are anticipating an unpleasant conversation, you can pretend to have it before it actually occurs. You can put it on a screen, sit in the movie theater and move to the projection booth, where you can analyze things rationally.

Even before the meeting, you can place the conflict in the proper perspective and consider your alternatives unemotionally. In fact, there is no reason to leave the projection booth. You can pretend to be there when the real conversation takes place. This will help you maintain perspective and control and remain calm and rational during the encounter.

SARA: *"Wouldn't you act strangely with the customer?"*

Maybe, but does that matter? You will be controlled and rational. If your customer is in *Hedonistic Self*, you are more likely to be able to apply the technique of *Hybrid Self* [*Chapter 3*] to reduce anger and increase rapport. The technique will work if you are calm and rational; it is less likely to work if you are angry, fearful or anxious.

❦ SUMMARY

Viewing an experience from another point of view can enrich awareness. You can do this in your imagination by performing certain exercises that either add or reduce the intensity of the experience.

> ROBERT: *"What are submodalities?"*
>
> Submodalities are aspects of a mental picture relating to
> context rather than to content. It would include qualities
> like size, location or clarity. Changing the submodalities
> can enrich or diminish your feelings about the experience
> being pictured and your degree of connection to it.

> DONNA: *"How do you see things from the customer's point of
> view?"*
>
> STEP 1: Create a vivid picture of the customer in your mind.
> STEP 2: Create a vivid picture of yourself in your mind.
> STEP 3: Picture yourself stepping into the customer so the
> customer is like a costume you are wearing.
> STEP 4: Become the customer. Feel the customer's sensa-
> tions and see the world through his eyes.
> STEP 5: Look at your product as the customer would. Be
> aware of the sensory elements (visual, auditory and kines-
> thetic) that might appeal to him.

> RITA: *"How can you distance yourself from a difficult memory or
> experience?"*
>
> You can distance yourself from a difficult memory or expe-
> rience by:
> STEP 1: Picturing yourself dealing with a difficult person or
> experience and putting the mental image on a movie screen.
> STEP 2: Seeing yourself sitting in the movie theater watching
> the argument on the screen.
> STEP 3: Seeing yourself in the projection booth looking at

yourself in the theater and at the screen on which you are having the argument.

Being in the projection booth — at a distance — will help you deal calmly and unemotionally with the situation so that you can think about alternatives and solutions in a rational way. If you anticipate a difficult conversation, you can create a mental picture and go to the projection booth before the event and stay there even during the encounter.

Getting Down to Business
in a Pleasant Sort of Way

YEARS AGO, MY PARTNER, MARC, CAME INTO MY OFFICE AND SAID: "NEIL, I KNOW YOU LOVE TO PLAY GOLF, AND I'M CONSIDERING TAKING LESSONS. WHAT DO YOU THINK?"

WELL, THIS WAS GOOD NEWS! IF I COULD GET MARC TO LEARN, THE TWO OF US COULD PLAY TOGETHER. I DESCRIBED THE JOY OF BEING OUTDOORS AND CONNECTING TO NATURE, THE FEELING OF HITTING THE BALL PERFECTLY AND SEEING IT FLOAT IN THE AIR AND SETTLE ON A GREEN EXPANSE OF FINELY CROPPED GRASS. HE PROBED MORE DEEPLY, AND I FOUND MYSELF THOROUGHLY LOST IN THE EXPERIENCE.

FINALLY, MARC SAID, "BOY, I FEEL REALLY GOOD LISTENING TO YOU." I TOLD HIM IT MADE ME FEEL GREAT TOO. "GOOD," HE SAID. "I JUST GOT A CALL FROM THE BANK. WE OVERDREW OUR ACCOUNT, AND THEY WANT TO TALK TO US. ARE YOU READY TO MAKE THE CALL?"

CHAPTER 7

Dealing with
Different Personalities

Developing strategies for dealing with different personality types will help you to build rapport effectively with a customer who may be very different from you.

ENRICHING AWARENESS

You can never completely share your customer's experience or understand his viewpoint. Rather, you must deduce his point of view by observing his behavior patterns, by inquiry and by comparing his actions with what you know of other people.

Through my observations and experience, I have developed models for identifying and categorizing common behavior patterns. Since I created them, these models are archetypes — theoretical personalities with a given set of values and common responses. Since they are constructs, no person's behavior will exactly fit any profile: the models merely summarize common modes of behavior. The models may help you grasp what is important to someone you do not immediately empathize with or understand. You should recognize aspects of each of the models within yourself. After all, we are each many people.

DIANE: *"What do you mean?"*
Are you the same with your parents as with your children?

Are you the same at a party with friends as when you're at a job interview? No, you are different people in different settings.

Remember the analogy I used earlier about going to a party? If you meet someone you don't like, you move on to successive people until you find someone you want to talk to. Selling is the opposite. To maximize success, you don't choose your customers; you make them want to choose you. Since you can't change the customer, you must identify and emphasize those elements of yourself that will be appealing to him. Fortunately, there are many "yous" to choose from. But you should make a conscious choice; don't fly on autopilot.

> DIANE: *"But that's ridiculous — you are who you are!"*
> Yes, but which one are you? Are you the one you are when you're with your parents, the one you are with your friends or the one you are at the office? You can de-emphasize the "you" that you would naturally fall into and consciously emphasize those aspects of yourself best suited to your customer. The key is to select the "you" that will help you build rapport.
> DIANE: *"Are you saying I have a shelf full of personas in my mind and should pick the one I think works best?"*
> Yes. The more flexible you are about adjusting your personality to the customer, the better you can build rapport.
> Let's consider the first personality model, the *Aristocrat*.

THE ARISTOCRAT

MY VALUES AND BELIEFS: My concern is for a certain group that I feel comfortable with and that I think understands what is important. I am aware that other people have different opinions, but they have their points of view, and I have mine.

MY BEHAVIORS: I prefer the manners and style of my group. If you are not part of that group, I will tend to ignore you unless I need something you have. In that case, I will be nice, but I will make you aware of who I am and who you are.

MY CRITERIA FOR CHANGE: I will change only if it furthers my status in the eyes of those important to me. If my pride is hurt, I won't change. I won't necessarily change just because I am wrong.

HOW I RESPOND TO PEOPLE WHO PRESSURE ME: I will be offended, and I will move on. I will not deal with them under any circumstances.

HOW I RESPOND TO PEOPLE WHO LIKE ME BUT WHOM I DO NOT LIKE: I smile at them and say very little. I tell them I am too busy to talk to them right now, I have another appointment.

HOW I RESPOND TO PEOPLE WHO TALK DOWN TO ME: I am deeply offended. How dare they!

HOW I RESPOND TO PEOPLE WHO TALK UP TO ME: I am pleased that they recognize my higher status. I like these people because they know their place and they will do what I tell them. If they do my bidding incorrectly, I will be offended, and they will apologize.

Okay, now we need someone to play the role. Diane, you play an Aristocrat selling her apartment. What price are you asking?

DIANE: "$3,000,000."

We have a buyer offering $2,000,000 who believes this is fair and that Diane is unrealistic. John, be the real estate broker trying to get Diane to reduce her price. You can each make up facts as you go along. John, I suggest you begin with "Do you have a minute?"

JOHN: *"Why 'Do you have a minute?'"*

You are submitting an offer and want her undivided attention. What if Diane is eating dinner with her family or busy with some other important task? If she won't be able to concentrate on what you are saying, you should ask what time would be better to call back.

JOHN: *"Hello, Diane, this is John from Bellmarc. Do you have a minute?"*

DIANE: *"What do you want?"*

JOHN: *"I want to talk to you about a buyer who saw your lovely apartment. I think he is interested."*

DIANE: *"Yes?"*

JOHN: *"He really liked it and made an offer of $2,000,000. I think you should consider it."*

DIANE: *"Do you? Well, I differ with that point of view."*

JOHN: *"Diane, he knows the market and what the apartment's worth. He can give you a quick deal; this is an opportunity."*

DIANE: *"I don't see any opportunity here. Goodbye."*

John, you started by being yourself. If you do that, you will communicate well with people like you, but you will have trouble with people who are not like you.

Try this: Create a picture in your mind of someone you think reflects the Aristocrat model. It could be someone you have known, a person you imagine or even a character from a movie. Look closely at the details of this picture to enrich the experience. Now create a second picture in your mind of yourself and see yourself stepping into the body of the Aristocrat as if you were putting on a costume. Feel his sensations and become that person, so you are looking out at the world from his perspective. Once you have done this, repeat the name of the personality type over and over again until you have it well connected in your memory as a resource. You can do this for each of the personality types.

JOHN: *"What's the benefit of this exercise?"*

You can communicate with your subconscious through mental pictures. By stepping into a mental picture of someone who conforms to this profile, you are telling your subconscious to apply all your knowledge that fits this model to you as you look through his eyes. You will gain a new awareness.

Do you have any comments about John's performance?

SARA: *"I would have said 'Mrs. Green' and 'John Belmont from Bellmarc' not 'Diane' and 'John.' I think the Aristocrat dislikes informality."*

I agree. It may be perceived as disrespect.

DONNA: *"I didn't like when John said, 'I think you should consider it.' Diane views him as a servant, and servants don't advise their masters."*

MICHAEL: *"John was condescending to her by saying, 'He knows the market.' This implied that Diane did not. John's general tone and rhythm were also dissimilar to hers."*

That's an important point. The problem was not just John's casualness and condescension but his failure to register her rhythm and to conform his style to fit hers.

Sara, why don't you try?

SARA: *"Hello, Mrs. Green? This is Sara Epstein from Bellmarc. Do you have a minute?"*

DIANE: *"Yes, just a minute."*

SARA: *"Oh, I'm sorry. Would you prefer that I call at a later time?"*

DIANE: *"No, no, it's fine. What do you want?"*

SARA: *"You know, I brought these absolutely fabulous people to your apartment. He's a famous doctor, very accomplished."*

DIANE: *"Yes? Who is he?"*

SARA: *"Dr. Smith, a well-known heart surgeon. Have you heard of him?"*

DIANE: *"No."*

SARA: *"Anyway, Dr. Smith is quite in love with your apartment and thought it would be great for his family."*

DIANE: *"I see."*

SARA: *"He made an offer. It's a little low, and I know you probably won't accept it, but I think it's a good starting point. He bid $2,000,000."*

DIANE: *"That's absurd. I have no interest in entertaining such an offer."*

SARA: *"I understand. However, I think it's worth at least considering. Why don't we make a counteroffer? Maybe he'll come up to an acceptable figure."*

Okay, let's stop. Michael, what did you think of Sara's performance?

MICHAEL: *"I was bothered by Sara's conversation about the doctor. I don't think an Aristocrat wants to be chatty with a salesperson."*

An Aristocrat will be chatty only with someone she perceives as an equal. Others should do her bidding. You can be chatty with an Aristocrat only if she opens the door by being chatty first.

DONNA: *"Sara seemed apologetic about the offer. She said it was no good before she even submitted it."*

SARA: *"Well, it was obviously too low."*

Who says it was too low? Just because the seller is asking more doesn't mean that any offer is too low. That is the seller's decision, not yours. You should submit the offer without reservations. If you apologize as you submit the offer, you are telling the seller not to take it seriously. It would have been better to say: "I have an offer for $2,000,000. How would you like me to proceed?"

DONNA: *"Sara also said, 'Why don't we make a counteroffer?' I don't think 'we' works well here."*

I agree. "We" implies a commonality of effort between the seller and the broker. The Aristocrat wants to be in control.

Now let me try.

Hi, Mrs. Green? This is Neil Binder from Bellmarc. Do you have a minute?

DIANE: *"Yes, what do you want?"*

I recently brought a couple to your apartment, and they were very impressed by the artwork in your living room. They directed me to compliment you on your taste and asked if you would be so kind as to tell them where you found such magnificent pieces.

DIANE: *"I got them directly from the artist. They are originals, you know, and very expensive."*

I understand. I am sure they recognized that. They also directed me to submit an offer on your apartment.

DIANE: *"I see. What is it?"*

I have been instructed to advise you that they would be willing to pay $2,000,000.

DIANE: *"That is far too low. Absolutely not."*

I understand. What instructions would you like to give me so that I can communicate how you feel on this matter?

DIANE: *"Tell them that if they want this apartment they must pay what it is worth. This is a Fifth Avenue apartment. The fire sales are elsewhere."*

I understand. Would you authorize me to give them a counteroffer of, perhaps, $2,500,000?

DIANE: *"No, that's too low. I am not interested in anything less than $3,000,000. That's what I want."*

I appreciate your giving me your time. I will be clear with them about your instructions, and if they have anything to say I will let you know immediately.

DIANE: *"Goodbye."*

Diane, how did my presentation compare with the others?

DIANE: *"In the other exercises I felt annoyed. I didn't get that feeling with you. I liked the compliments. The affirmation that I have good taste and owned valuable things made me feel special. I also liked the fact that it was the buyer complimenting me and not you."*

Yes, in the eyes of the Aristocrat my opinions are meaningless. That I was "directed," my actions were "authorized" and I sought "instructions" meant that I was acting properly as a servant. In dealing with an Aristocrat, it is key to remember that she views people as being "in the club" or "not in the club."

A Bellmarc salesperson once had a good offer on an apartment, but every time he called the Aristocratic seller, the seller would say, "I'm busy now" and hang up. My partner, Marc, came up with a plan. He told the salesperson to say, "Mr. Smith, the president of Bellmarc would like to speak to you." When he did, the seller said: "Hold on. I want to go to my den."

When the seller picked up the phone, he immediately said to Marc,

"Did you know that I am a member of the St. Tropez Club?" Well, by luck, Marc knew of this club, which is located in the South of France. He said: "Really? What a wonderful club!" and talked about the club's restaurant, yachts and goings-on in the area. After a while, the Aristocrat said: "Look, about the apartment, tell your salesperson that I will sell to his customer. I will have my lawyer call him."

There was no negotiated price! Marc had succeeded because the seller perceived him as being part of his "club" and someone he would deal with. Since Marc was part of the accepted group, he would know what was appropriate to do.

> Do you think an Aristocrat has to be wealthy?
>
> MICHAEL: *"Yes."*
>
> Not so. An Aristocrat is anyone who is on the inside while you are on the outside. It is not necessarily a money issue. Say that I am a dedicated member of Zeta Beta Tau fraternity and you are not. If that is my club, the same rules apply. The club could be any group that the Aristocrat brings into the decision-making process. It might even be an ethnicity, culture, religion or race; whenever a customer looks at people as being "in" or "out" of his group, the profile applies.

The Investment Banker

MY VALUES AND BELIEFS: Life is a battle and survival goes to the fittest. Everything has a risk/return trade-off. I measure the probabilities of success using concise data. I believe that people, like machines, are assets. They each have ways of producing results.

MY BEHAVIORS: People are either potential clients or employees. I treat potential clients as comrades. I issue orders to employees. My actions focus on getting things done. I size people up to determine how to get them to produce the results I want.

MY CRITERIA FOR CHANGE: I am always evaluating the risk/return trade-offs and will be flexible if the situation requires it. I will listen to other people unless I view them as emotional or they can't get to the point. Emotional people annoy me, and people who cannot get to the point waste my time. Neither has anything to say as far as I am concerned.

HOW I RESPOND TO PEOPLE WHO PRESSURE ME: These people are fools. Do they think they are dealing with a jerk? I will play that game, and I will win and they will never forget it.

HOW I RESPOND TO PEOPLE WHO LIKE ME BUT WHOM I DO NOT LIKE: They annoy me. I try to avoid them. I smile and say something pleasant, then move on as quickly as possible.

HOW I RESPOND TO PEOPLE WHO TALK DOWN TO ME: I get angry. Who do they think they are? I tend to stare at them and say nothing or very little. I feel like I want to destroy them.

HOW I RESPOND TO PEOPLE WHO TALK UP TO ME: Don't flatter me. I hate to be flattered. These people just waste my time. If you have a purpose, get to the point.

Jonathan, you be the Investment Banker. What price do you want for your apartment?

JONATHAN: *"$800,000."*

Good, we have an offer of $650,000. Donna, you submit the offer as the broker.

DONNA: *"Hello, Mr. Walker? This is Donna Rissota from Bellmarc. Do you have a minute?*

JONATHAN: *"Yes, what is it?"*

DONNA: *"I have some good news for you. I brought a lovely couple to your apartment, and they were overjoyed with the views. They're very excited about it."*

JONATHAN: *"I see. Did they make an offer?"*

DONNA: *"Yes, they did, and I think we should consider it as a good beginning. They want the apartment, and they are prepared to be fair."*

JONATHAN: *"What's the offer?"*

DONNA: *"Well, I thought you might like to hear a little about them."*

JONATHAN: *"Look, will you tell me the number already, I'm in a hurry."*

DONNA: *"$650,000."*

JONATHAN: *"The answer is no. Goodbye."*

Okay, what did you think about this conversation?

SARA: *"I could feel the ice running through Jonathan's veins. He didn't give her a break!"*

JONATHAN: *"I was annoyed. Donna wanted to be friendly, and I wanted to get the job done. She was wasting my time."*

SARA: *"Jonathan didn't want to learn anything about these buyers; all he wanted was the number. Maybe Donna should have given it to him right away."*

If she had, what would have happened?

DONNA: *"He would have said no, and there would have been no further discussion."*

Maybe, but he wants to sell the apartment. You might have been able to get "instructions" about how to proceed.

MICHAEL: *"I thought the word 'fair' was ineffective. When Sara said that, Jonathan seemed to smirk."*

JONATHAN: *"I wanted concrete information and results. 'Fair' was not relevant."*

Okay, let me take a shot.

Hi, Jonathan? This is Neil Binder from Bellmarc. Do you have a minute?

JONATHAN: *"Just a minute."*

Would you rather I call you later?

JONATHAN: *"No, no, what do you want?"*

I just received an offer on your apartment in the amount of $650,000. How would you like me to proceed?

JONATHAN: *"Tell them no."*

I see. The buyer told me he is considering your apartment and another, similar in size to yours, in the building directly across the street. He can purchase that one for $700,000, and it has a lower maintenance than yours, but it doesn't have as good a view and he likes your building better. I believe he would prefer yours if you would give him a similar price.

JONATHAN: *"$700,000? Let him buy the other apartment."*

I understand. I know you know the value of your apartment and the market. Could you give me some information to convince the buyer that your apartment is worth $800,000? If I can get those facts, maybe he would see the logic of your position.

JONATHAN: *"That's your job, not mine."*

That's true. However, you must have information I don't, because according to my records $700,000 seems reasonable, and obviously I'm mistaken.

JONATHAN: *"I suggest that you tell him I would consider $750,000. Get back to me with his response."*

Yes, sir. Goodbye.

Here's my strategy: Since the Investment Banker is focused on the employer/employee relationship, I try to be a good employee and present concrete information that he can analyze efficiently and effectively.

I did not use "Mr.," though I fully identified myself. It is customary in today's business world for people to address one another by first names. If I knew that Jonathan was significantly older than I, I would have used the salutation.

I quickly presented the offer and asked, "How would you like me to proceed?" That is a good phrase because it makes the seller act as an employer, giving instructions for further action.

Then I presented the facts, describing another product the buyer might choose so the seller could evaluate the risk/return relationship and weigh the alternatives. I gave him the price and facts, good and bad. The information seemed more credible because it was not one-sided.

Since I disagreed with the seller's conclusion, I asked for facts supporting his decision, deferring to him and his knowledge. I effectively said, "Since you are the employer, you must know better, and I must be mistaken." This validated him, but also made him support his conclusion. I was really saying, "Prove it to me." If he could, I could give that information to the buyer. In this case, I called his bluff and forced him to agree to a lower figure.

DONNA: *"I felt that you were in the army talking to a general. You even ended with 'sir.'"*

I looked at it that way as well, and I said "sir" very purposefully. I want the Investment Banker to know that I respect him as the leader and my superior in this mission.

SARA: *"Don't you think you could have loosened him up and maybe tried to create a relationship?"*

He's the customer, and I must do this on his terms, or he will find another salesperson. If he accepts me as a valuable employee, he will open up to me. I must first respect him, then earn his respect.

SAM: *"Didn't you risk annoying him and making him defensive by bringing up the buyer's other alternative?"*

Yes, particularly if he viewed me as opposing him. That's why I said that the buyer had communicated this to me; I was just passing along information. There was no threat, just a choice.

SAM: *"What if there is no alternative present?"*

Then I ask the Investment Banker how he arrived at his valuation. Once he tells me that, I'll know how committed he is to his asking price.

The Robber Baron

MY VALUES AND BELIEFS: I like to play. Business is a game to me, part of the game of life. I like my friends, and my friends like me. I like to help people because it makes me feel both good and important. I have a clear sense of how things work. It's all about playing by the rules.

MY BEHAVIORS: I like to make my presence felt. I think about you while I talk to you and judge your actions as right or wrong. I insist that you see things my way. I like my family; I like to show them off and talk about them.

MY CRITERIA FOR CHANGE: I will change, but change takes time for me. If I have no choice, I will do what you want. This is not change — this is the nature of the game of life.

HOW I RESPOND TO PEOPLE WHO PRESSURE ME: I defend myself. I won't bend to pressure — pressure must be met with pressure.

HOW I RESPOND TO PEOPLE WHO LIKE ME BUT WHOM I DO NOT LIKE: I try to persuade them to change and see another perspective. I imply that their reward will be that I will like them.

HOW I RESPOND TO PEOPLE WHO TALK DOWN TO ME: I talk down to

---

them and defend myself. I argue and make them see why they don't make sense.

HOW I RESPOND TO PEOPLE WHO TALK UP TO ME: I like this. I am a winner. I'll ask them about certain topics to see if we are on the same team. If we are, maybe we can have fun together.

Michael, you be our Robber Baron. What are you asking for your apartment?

MICHAEL: *"$750,000."*

Okay, the offer is $650,000. Cassandra, you be the broker.

CASSANDRA: *"Hi, this is Cassandra Martinez from Bellmarc. Do you have a minute?"*

MICHAEL: *"Well, hello, Cassandra Martinez from Bellmarc. Of course I have a minute — for you. So, speak! What's new in the world of real estate?"*

CASSANDRA: *"I have an offer on your apartment, sir. They bid $650,000."*

MICHAEL: *"That sounds rather low, don't you think?"*

CASSANDRA: *"How would you like me to proceed?"*

MICHAEL: *"Well, why don't you proceed to get me more money? That sounds like a good way to proceed."*

CASSANDRA: *"Is there anything I should tell the buyer?"*

MICHAEL: *"I guess you could tell them to pay more."*

CASSANDRA: *"I see. I'll tell the buyer and see what I can do."*

Did you notice that Michael was playing with you?

CASSANDRA: *"It was frustrating. He was always toying with me."*

SAM: *"The Robber Baron seems to like to twist words. When Cassandra asked him how to 'proceed,' he played with the word rather than responding substantively."*

Yes, Robber Barons treat life as a game. In fact, the language of games is an effective way of creating a connection.

SAM: *"Cassandra was too serious. She went straight to the point, and the Robber Baron beat her up for it."*

When talking to Robber Barons, you must get into a rhythm. They are dancing even when they sit still. Timing matters — Robber Barons love momentum. When someone is playing with you, why don't you play back?

Let me try.

Hi, Michael, it's Neil Binder from Bellmarc. Do you have a minute?

MICHAEL: *"Sure, what's up?"*

I got a nibble that I think we can bring in, and I want to talk to you about it.

MICHAEL: *"What do you have?"*

A family struggling to make it, looking for a chance.

MICHAEL: *"So, let's give them a chance. What's their offer?"*

They came to me with $650,000.

MICHAEL: *"You call that a nibble? I think it's more of a look!"*

Okay, I'll buy that. But I still think we can get them to bite. They are willing to do a fair deal, and I know you are too. They just don't want to be taken advantage of. They don't have a lot of money and are relying on me to help them do the right thing.

MICHAEL: *"Okay, what do you want me to say?"*

I want you to throw them a straight ball down the middle and tell them you will do $700,000.

MICHAEL: *"Not going to happen. I don't think that's a straight ball; I think that's a sucker pitch. That's not the way I work."*

So tell me what to do here.

MICHAEL: *"Have them come up. I want more money."*

They understand that they have a responsibility, and I believe they will do the right thing. Will you play at $725,000?

MICHAEL: *"If they are willing to step up to the plate and say that, I will consider it."*

Okay, let's stop here.

I want to give you a few pointers. Robber Barons love to talk in terms of the game. Robber Barons are like car dealers. When they sell cars they "score." When they meet, it's for a golf outing or at the racetrack. They like contests and talk about being "on the team" and "winning." However, Robber Barons don't only want to make a deal; they want a story along with the sale. Sometimes the story is more important than the sale itself. Anyone who loves the game of business and sees the sale as an opportunity to play fits this profile. The Robber Baron likes to do things with finesse.

> CASSANDRA: *"You highlighted the word 'responsibility.' That doesn't sound like a game word to me."*
>
> The Robber Baron looks at fairness and responsibility as all part of fair play and one of the rules of the game. Notice I also used "we." Unlike with the Investment Banker or the Aristocrat, using "we" works for a Robber Baron. It puts you on his team.

The Best Buddy

MY VALUES AND BELIEFS: I view the world as a little overwhelming. I am insecure about where I fit in, particularly if I am doing something new. I believe that people are fundamentally either good or bad.

MY BEHAVIORS: Being liked validates my self-worth. Dealing with caring people is important to me. I like to talk about caring and to be cared for. I am not necessarily weak, but my strength is in my tolerance for what other people do. I will tolerate a lot if I see you as a good person. I will tolerate little if I see you as a bad person. I can be emotional.

MY CRITERIA FOR CHANGE: I appreciate information from someone helping me. A good person's information is reason to consider changing. I want to please, but I must remember that it is my life.

HOW I RESPOND TO PEOPLE WHO PRESSURE ME: I am very uncomfortable. I wonder if this person is pressuring me because he cares about me and wants to protect me or because he is trying to take advantage of me.

HOW I RESPOND TO PEOPLE WHO LIKE ME BUT WHOM I DO NOT LIKE: I distrust their motives. They want to take advantage of me, and I have nothing to say to them. I wish I could run away.

HOW I RESPOND TO PEOPLE WHO TALK DOWN TO ME: They are like my parents. I will be embarrassed or attentive or, if they exceed my threshold, assertive and defensive.

HOW I RESPOND TO PEOPLE WHO TALK UP TO ME: They are like my younger brother or sister. I will protect and help them. I am generous and loyal to them.

Donna, you be our Best Buddy. What are you asking for your apartment?

DONNA: *"$500,000."*

And we have an offer of $400,000. Sara, you be the broker.

SARA: *"Hi, Donna, this is Sara from Bellmarc. Do you have a minute?"*

DONNA: *"Sure. How are you today?"*

SARA: *"I'm fine, thank you. Donna, I have an offer on your apartment, and I want to talk to you about it. The buyers really like it, but they think it is priced a bit high. They offered $400,000."*

DONNA: *"I see. That seems a little low."*

SARA: *"Well, your price might be a little high. I feel their offer is a good one."*

DONNA: *"You do?"*

SARA: *"I'm in the market every day, Donna, and you can trust me. The price you are asking is too high. You have to be more reasonable."*

DONNA: *"But other people have told me it's reasonable."*

SARA: *"Did they bring you any offers? I'm coming with real buyers, and I think they are ready to move right away. I don't think you should lose them."*

DONNA: *"I don't know. Let me think about it."*

SARA: *"I recommend you don't take too long, okay?"*

DONNA: *"I just want to think about it."*

Good. John, what did you notice about this conversation?

JOHN: *"Donna was shutting down. Sara came on strong, and Donna kind of went into her hole. Donna didn't trust Sara and was afraid of her."*

MICHAEL: *"Sara was telling her what to do without any sympathy for her feelings. Sara was trying to railroad her."*

And as a result, Donna just said she would think about it. That is a typical Best Buddy response. They don't tell you what they're thinking; they just run away.

The Best Buddy can be a vacillator. He is intensely connected to feelings. When communicating with a Best Buddy, concentrate your energy in your chest. Connect to your feelings and try to empathize with his. A Best Buddy needs an emotional connection to feel good about the process. He is entering unknown waters and is looking for a lifeguard. He wants you to lead him into the water and reassure him that everything is all right and that "we are doing this together." If something doesn't feel right, the Best Buddy can lose trust and shut the door on a deal.

JOHN: *"Is a Best Buddy a first-time buyer?"*

Possibly, but it's a pattern displayed by even knowledgeable buyers. The Best Buddy may also be protecting someone else. Either way, focus your energy in your chest, communicate feelings and respect the Best Buddy's need for trust and reassurance.

Now I'll try.

Hi, Donna, it's Neil. Do you have a minute?

DONNA: *"Yes, of course!"*

I just got off the phone with my buyer. She made an offer.

DONNA: *"Is it a good offer?"*

The offer is $400,000.

DONNA: *"That doesn't sound very good."*

I guess not. I know this is a big decision; I understand. Whatever you decide, I know you are doing the right thing. This is really important.

DONNA: *"Yes, it is, isn't it? What do you think I should do?"*

I have to give you advice, and I will, but I want to remind you, Donna, that as a real estate broker I get paid when you do a deal. I make money if you do this, I can't remove that part of my job.

DONNA: *"I appreciate your letting me know."*

Thank you. I just want to do what is right.

DONNA: *"I understand."*

I think the buyers are a little afraid of such a big commitment. This is a big decision for them too. We have to respect that, and yet they have to pay more. I propose that we offer to split the difference and ask for $450,000. I think that is fair and they should take it.

DONNA: *"I'll have to think about it."*

I know. This is a big decision. I know you have to consider this on your own.

Let me explain my strategy. Since the Best Buddy is looking for someone to trust and connect with, I started by introducing myself informally and then validating the magnitude of her decision. I want her to feel that I respect her process. Second, I reminded her of my self-interest.

SARA: *"Why would you do that?"*

Because the Best Buddy already knows my role. By reminding her of my interest, I affirmed my trustworthiness. That in itself is a validation that builds a connection.

SARA: *"But you did not get her to commit to the deal."*

No, but since I knew she might want to consider it on her own, I didn't press for immediate action. Best Buddies run away from pressure and move toward people they think care and are "real." I presented a "fair" deal and characterized the buyers as "afraid," implying that "they are just like you, so we have to work together." That may work a lot better than saying the buyer is sophisticated.

Remember to speak from your chest. Best Buddies are often very kinesthetic. They want to connect with you and feel good about talking to you, so you must feel good about talking to them as well. Sincerity is important.

SARA: *"Why were you so specific about the price?"*

As a professional, you must be prepared to give specific

advice, particularly when asked. Being vague says that you are unsure about what to do. If you are unsure, how can you educate your customer? Take a position and spell out your assumptions and reasons. The Best Buddy needs advice and will respond to your leadership. You are the lifeguard, and you know the way. Phrases like "that depends" only add to his anxiety and make him not trust you.

SARA: *"But what if your advice is wrong?"*

Then apologize and correct your error as soon as you become aware of it. You can always get out of the truth; you can never get out of a lie. If you are unsure, you can hedge with phrases like "my best estimate," "within a range of" or "given conditions as I see them today." You are the lifeguard: you must advise the Best Buddy how to swim.

SARA: *"Since this call was inconclusive, what do you do now?"*

Give the Best Buddy a reasonable amount of time, then call back. When you do, be careful to minimize the pressure. A good strategy is to say, "The buyer just called and wanted me to contact you so he can decide what to do." Another good strategy is to say: "I know this is a big decision. I am calling to see if there is anything I can do to help you." Either of these is better than saying, "Did you decide yet?"

The Expert

MY VALUES AND BELIEFS: I believe that knowledge is the key to decision-making. The most knowledgeable person will be the most competent and should be the one making a decision.

MY BEHAVIORS: I respect people who know what they are doing, and I feel comfortable taking their lead. However, before I trust them, I test their knowledge against mine. If they don't measure up, forget it! I am shocked by the number of ignorant people I run into and how many lack basic common sense. I often have to take over even when I don't want to because nobody else is qualified.

MY CRITERIA FOR CHANGE: I change when new information logically demands it. I am impressed by someone who can teach me something and will try to learn as much as I can from him.

HOW I RESPOND TO PEOPLE WHO PRESSURE ME: They have a lot of nerve! Who do they think they are talking to? These people are idiots who don't know what they are talking about.

HOW I RESPOND TO PEOPLE WHO LIKE ME BUT WHOM I DO NOT LIKE: I pretend I am listening, though not very well. I correct their errors and smirk at their stupidity. They make me numb.

HOW I RESPOND TO PEOPLE WHO TALK DOWN TO ME: I become defensive and must prove my worth. They aren't as smart as they think they are, and I will expose them.

HOW I RESPOND TO PEOPLE WHO TALK UP TO ME: I feel this is appropriate since I know more than they do. I might even teach them something — they might be good students.

Ken, you play the Expert. What price do you want?

KEN: *"$2,000,000."*

Okay, we have an offer of $1,350,000. Susan, why don't you be the broker?

SUSAN: *"Hi, Ken, this is Susan from Bellmarc. Do you have a minute?"*

KEN: *"Yes, I do."*

SUSAN: *"I received an offer on your apartment and would like to talk to you about it."*

KEN: *"I see. What is the offer?"*

SUSAN: *"$1,350,000."*

KEN: *"That is unacceptable. Did you qualify these buyers?"*

SUSAN: *"Of course. They can afford it."*

KEN: *"Then why are they bidding so low? You should have been able to show them the value. Why are you presenting me with this ridiculous offer?"*

SUSAN: *"Well, it's a start. I thought you might consider a counteroffer."*

KEN: *"To that? Are you kidding? Don't you know your job? That's not how you do this. You get them to offer something relative to the market. Why am I dealing with you? You don't seem to understand what you're doing!"*

SUSAN: *"I'm sorry, sir. I'm doing my best."*

Let's stop here. What did you think about Susan's performance?

SARA: *"She got defensive and lost any sense of what to do. Once you say you're sorry to this kind of seller, you're sunk."*

Yes and no. Yes if you continue to assert your authority; no if you defer to the Expert and take on the student role. To the Expert, you have just proved your incompetence. If your apology says: "I'm sorry I disappointed you. I know you are sophisticated, so I am happy to take your lead," it might work, since the Expert wants to take control anyway. However, the kind of sorry that means, "I'm sorry, but I'm just doing my job" will weaken your position. You have neither acquiesced to the Expert's authority nor proved your worth. The Expert will only get angry with you.

SUSAN: *"I felt like I was being scolded. I was getting pretty angry, though I tried to hold it in."*

The Expert is looking to kick you. He wants to prove his

superiority and have you acknowledge his greater competence. Even the slightest misstep can meet with incredible abuse. Once you said the buyer was qualified, which was a perfectly reasonable thing to say, you were set up for the kill. You should have explained how you ascertained that the buyer was qualified, showing that you went through a procedure the Expert could affirm. He may be condescending, but you have to stand your ground and give him verifiable and quantifiable facts to prove your competence.

Okay, let me take a shot.

Hi, Mr. Smith, this is Neil Binder from Bellmarc. Do you have a minute?

KEN: *"Yes, what is it?"*

Sir, I just received an offer of $1,350,000 for your apartment. How would you like me to proceed?

KEN: *"$1,350,000? That is absurd. Don't you know how to do your job? That is not a real offer. What are you doing?"*

I understand your anger. I, too, found the offer unacceptable. However, I know that you are very knowledgeable, and I didn't want to take any liberties without first consulting with you.

KEN: *"I see. Well, you haven't done your job. You let the buyer believe it is acceptable to make an absurd bid. You may have placed the deal in jeopardy. Do you know that?"*

I understand. However, with your help this problem can be resolved. I have information in my listing book, which I am happy to show you, on five comparable properties that suggest a value of $1,500,000 for your apartment. It would have been inappropriate for me to present this to the buyers, since you know the value is $2,000,000. Could you give me the additional information you have to justify the

$2,000,000 price so I can transmit it to the buyers? I know
that with your assistance I can persuade them to come up.

KEN: *"It is your job to get that information, not mine."*

I understand, but my information is incomplete. It shows a
value of only $1,500,000. I need the information on which
you based the $2,000,000 price. Can you assist me?

Okay. Let's discuss my strategy. I did not fight the Expert but affirmed
his superior knowledge by asking for his help. However, I came prepared for his attack and presented specific information supporting my
valuation of $1,500,000.

He knew I did my homework, and that neutralized his antagonism.
Now he had to prove that he knew more than I. If he did so, then I would
continue to act as his student. If he couldn't, then he would accept my
competence and I would become a compatriot. I like to think of the
Expert as a subset of the Aristocrat whose club is the "club of knowledge," of which you are either a member or an outsider.

SARA: *"You asked for information justifying his position as you
did with the Investment Banker. Is that a standard strategy?"*

Yes. Don't think you have all the answers. Be prepared to
learn from your customer. If he has information you don't,
you can learn from him. If he doesn't, you should know
that, too. Bluffing is a common sales technique. Find out
if your customer's poker hand is good or bad.

❧ REMAINING ISSUES

JANE: *"What if I can't think of anyone who fits one of your personality models to do the mental exercise of stepping into his
body and seeing through his eyes?"*

Try to categorize people you know based on their most prominent traits. When you have accumulated a few people who fit that model, merge them into a single person in your mind. Create an imaginary composite person.

JANE: *"In each of the examples, the negotiation was with the seller. Is it different with a buyer?"*

No. Both need to be persuaded to accept your position.

ℳℴ SUMMARY

The personality models described in this chapter are tools to help you build rapport with customers who are different from you. The key is to identify the customer's pattern and conform your approach to match his. You can give the same information in many different ways — choose the method most likely to get through to your particular customer.

DIANE: *"What is the Aristocrat's pattern, and how do you respond?"*

Pattern: You are either in or out of the customer's "club."

Response: Servant to master.

JOHN: *"What is the Investment Banker's pattern, and how do you respond?"*

Pattern: Purchase decisions are made on the basis of data quantifying the risk/return trade-offs.

Response: Employee to employer.

CAROL: *"What is the Robber Baron's pattern, and how do you respond?"*

Pattern: Negotiating is a game.

Response: Be on the team.

DONNA: *"What is the Best Buddy's pattern, and how do you respond?"*

Pattern: Advice must be from someone trustworthy.

Response: Connectedness.

SYLVIA: *"What is the* Expert's *pattern, and how do you respond?"*

Pattern: The most knowledgeable person should make the decision.

Response: Student to teacher.

JOAN: *"How do you use these models in selling?"*

First look for the customer's primary pattern. Then identi-fy the approach that will enrich communication and be persuasive. You should choose your approach deliberately rather than reflexively.

ARLENE: *"What if the customer doesn't perfectly match the personality profile?"*

Nobody ever does. These are common patterns that I have observed. They are not meant to describe any individual. However, each customer will resemble one model more than the others. Selecting the closest model and con-sciously choosing your approach will enhance your chances of getting information across to that customer effectively.

❀

Being the Right Kind of Person
at the Right Time

ONCE THERE WAS A RICE FARMER. HE WOULD LEAVE HIS HOME EARLY EVERY MORNING TO TEND HIS CROP, MAKING SURE THAT THE ROWS OF SLENDER PLANTS WERE WELL MAINTAINED AND PROPERLY COVERED IN WATER. HE WAS ALWAYS REWARDED WITH A FINE HARVEST, AND THE OTHER FARMERS ADMIRED HIM.

STILL, HE WAS UNHAPPY, SO HE LOOKED FOR GREATER OPPORTUNITY IN AMERICA, BELIEVING THAT HE COULD SUCCEED THERE IN WHATEVER HE PLANTED. HE PURCHASED SOME GOOD LAND AND PLANTED CORN.

HE WORKED VERY HARD THAT FIRST YEAR, YET HIS CROP WAS A FAILURE. ON HIS NEIGHBOR'S FARM, THE STALKS STOOD TALL, AND THE EARS OF CORN WERE JUICY AND GOLDEN.

THE NEXT YEAR HE WORKED EVEN HARDER, YET HE WAS AGAIN DISAPPOINTED. SO HE SWALLOWED HIS PRIDE AND WENT TO HIS NEIGHBOR. IN ANGUISH, HE SAID: "I AM A FAILURE. I CANNOT GROW CORN LIKE YOU." THE NEIGHBOR REPLIED, "DID YOU ASK YOUR CORN WHY IT IS UNHAPPY?"

THE FARMER DIDN'T UNDERSTAND AND SAID: "BUT CORN CAN'T TALK!" THE NEIGHBOR SAID: "OF COURSE IT CAN. HOW CAN YOU LOVE SOMETHING YOU CAN'T TALK TO? I LOVE MY CORN, AND MY CORN LOVES ME!"

THEN THE FARMER REMEMBERED HOW HE HAD LOVED HIS RICE. HE REMEMBERED THE GENTLE TOUCH OF THE PLANTS AND THE WARM FEELING OF THE WATER KISSING THE ROOTS UNDER HIS FEET. HE REMEMBERED THE PRIDE HE FELT AS THE RICE GREW PLENTIFULLY OVER HIS LAND.

AS HE THOUGHT ABOUT FARMING CORN, HE REALIZED THAT

EVERYTHING HE DID WAS BASED ON HOW HE HAD FARMED RICE. HE HAD NEVER LOOKED AT CORN FOR ITS OWN SAKE, BUT ONLY THOUGHT ABOUT HOW CORN WAS DIFFERENT FROM HIS BELOVED RICE. THE FARMER THEN ASKED HIMSELF, HOW DOES CORN WORK? HE DIDN'T KNOW. IN HIS ANGER, HE STOOD TALL LIKE THE CORN AND YELLED: "CORN, THIS IS FATHER FARMER! I AM TIRED OF BEING HUMBLE TO YOU."

AS HE STOOD TALL AND CONTINUED TO SHOUT, HE FELT A SENSATION THAT HE COULDN'T EXPLAIN — SOMETHING WAS HAPPENING. SUDDENLY HE UNDERSTOOD: YOU MUST BEND OVER RICE AND GIVE IT NURTURING LOVE; THE HEART OF RICE IS LOW TO THE GROUND. CORN STANDS TALL; THE HEART OF CORN IS IN THE SKY. YOU CANNOT BE HUMBLE TO CORN; YOU MUST LOOK UP AND SPEAK PROUDLY TO THE SWAYING STALKS FILLED WITH GOLDEN SWEETNESS.

HOW DIFFERENT THEY ARE! IT TAKES TWO DIFFERENT TYPES OF FARMERS, SPEAKING FROM THE HEART, TO FIND THE SPECIAL MESSAGE IN EACH CROP. THE FARMER SMILED IN SATISFACTION. NOW HE KNEW THE SECRETS OF BOTH AND COULD BE THE RIGHT FARMER FOR HIS TALL, BOLD CORN JUST AS HE HAD BEEN FOR THE HUMBLE RICE.

CHAPTER 8

ℳ

Creating an Effective Sales Strategy

In order to succeed at sales, you must have a strategy. You must understand where you want to go and what obstacles are blocking your path and why. Then you must gather information and take action to address those obstacles to achieve your objective.

ℳ THE COMPETITIVE SALES ENVIRONMENT

In selling, it is important to have a strategy in order to serve your customer in an efficient, effective manner. A salesperson must plan carefully to respond fully to the specific needs of each individual.

In a competitive environment, how do you gain an edge?

TOM: *"You need to be first with the information, the first at bat."*

Yes, but it isn't enough. What you say is more important.

SARA: *"You need to say the things the customer wants to hear."*

Yes, but within the bounds of honesty and sincerity. If I wanted an exclusive agreement to sell a house, I might tell the owners I liked it even if I didn't. However, if it was worth $300,000, and they wanted to hear that it was worth $500,000, I would not lie to get them to enter into an agreement. The first is puffery; the second is deceit.

RITA: *"You need to build rapport."*

Yes. But even if I like you, I may lack confidence in your ability to serve my interest. You must also prove your competence as an authority. Rapport and authority together create the foundation for credibility and trust.

Once you have established both rapport and credibility, however, you still need a concrete plan for overcoming obstacles and attaining your goal: a sales strategy.

The Key Points of an Effective Sales Strategy: "Only I WIN"

O is for OBJECTIVES. Be clear about what you want.

I is for ISSUES. Identify the obstacles to be overcome.

W is for WHY. Understand the underlying reasons behind the issues.

I is for INFORMATION. Identify essential information.

N is for NEXT. Determine the next step to be taken.

"O" Is for OBJECTIVES

✺ UNDERSTANDING "O" FOR OBJECTIVES

You must be a clear about what you want to achieve. One way of clarifying the objective is to see it. Picture yourself achieving your desired outcome.

JOHN: *"What if the customer changes what he wants?"*

Then your objective changes. One of the worst things a salesperson can do is become so committed to an objective that he is unable to adjust when the situation changes. You should step back and reevaluate often during the sales process.

You are always working with several objectives over a span of time. A short-term objective would be to persuade a buyer to purchase a *given property*; a medium-term objective would be to sell him *any property*; a long-term objective would be to *fulfill life goals*. You might need to change a shorter-term objective in order to improve your chances of achieving a long-term goal. Long-term objectives are the most meaningful; they underlie all our actions.

Say you are running in a long-distance cross-country race. Your long-term objective is to be an accomplished athlete; your medium-term term objective is to win this race; your short-term objective is to avoid the pitfalls along the path you are on.

For each objective, you should see a picture, and each has its own obstacles to be overcome if you want to move successively from one to the other. If you trip and sprain your ankle, you may fail in your short- and medium-term objectives, but your long-term objective remains intact. Your new short-term goal may be to do rehabilitative exercises. You can see your leg becoming strong and healthy again so you can run in the next race. If you were unable to adjust your short-term goal and strategy, you could lose the long-term goal as well. When you get new information, rethink your choices. To choose to stay the course or change direction should be an active decision not a passive one.

❧ SHORT-TERM OBJECTIVES: THE CUSTOMER'S BUYING FORMULA

In any sales relationship, the buyer's short-term objective is satisfying specific needs with the item being purchased, and your short-term objective is to satisfy the customer. The buyer has a set of preconceived notions of what he wants, which he interprets into a *Buying Formula*. The Buying Formula is expressed in nouns and focuses on three elements: *quality* (which includes image), *utility* (i.e., how well the product serves his needs) and *cost*.

The customer evaluates the relative merits of each component to find the product with the best quality and utility at the lowest cost. Your goal is to learn about the customer's needs and then to educate him in order to persuade him to make a decision so that you can profit.

> Arlene, pretend you want to buy an apartment. What kind do you want?
>
> ARLENE: *"A two-bedroom."*
>
> Why?
>
> ARLENE: *"My husband and I have a young son, so I want a bedroom for him and one for ourselves."*
>
> Okay, what else would you like?
>
> ARLENE: *"I want as much space as I can get for $500,000."*
>
> Does the location matter?
>
> ARLENE: *"I prefer the East Side of Manhattan. I have a lot of friends there."*
>
> Do you prefer a particular kind of building?
>
> ARLENE: *"I want a doorman — I want to feel safe."*
>
> Does it matter how the apartment is laid out?
>
> ARLENE: *"Not really, but I would like it to feel open."*
>
> Would you live on a second floor?
>
> ARLENE: *"That would be too noisy. I want something higher up and quiet."*
>
> What about a view?
>
> ARLENE: *"I don't want a dark apartment. That seems scary to me. I want light."*
>
> I know you care about space. Is that the most important thing to you?

ARLENE: *"Yes, I want the most space I can get within my budget. I wouldn't want to have to move again if we have another child. Space is really important."*

Arlene, would you say that your immediate goal is to spend $500,000 to get a bright, spacious two-bedroom apartment on the East Side of Manhattan in a doorman building on at least a middle-level floor?

ARLENE: *"Yes."*

Good, that is your basic Buying Formula. I can now probe for greater specificity on each element to get a richer picture of what you want. I could do this for any product, service or idea — identify the customer's Buying Formula, then probe further to enrich my understanding.

❧ MEDIUM-TERM OBJECTIVES: THE BUYER'S PURCHASING CRITERIA

The Buying Formula is a set of considerations — nouns — for comparing one product with another. Underlying these nouns are verbs that tell why the buyer is making his decisions. For example, a buyer may want space to entertain, to have children or to work from home. There are many possibilities. These motivations are his *Purchasing Criteria*. Satisfying the Purchasing Criteria is the buyer's medium-term objective.

Arlene, what are your hopes in buying an apartment?

ARLENE: *"I hope to get a lot of space."*

Why?

ARLENE: *"Because that will help me cope with my family."*

So you want *to cope*. Do you have any more hopes?

ARLENE: *"I want a space big enough so that I can have another child."*

So you hope *to have another child*. Do you have any other hopes?

ARLENE: *"I would like to make more friends. I have some friends on the East Side, and I would like to make more."*

So you hope *to make friends*. Anything else?

ARLENE: *"I hope to get a good deal."*

Why?

ARLENE: *"So I can save money. I want to be careful."*

So you want *to save*?

ARLENE: *"Yes."*

Anything else?

ARLENE: *"No, that's about it."*

Do you have any fears about buying an apartment?

ARLENE: *"Yes, I am concerned about safety."*

So you want *to be safe*. Any others?

ARLENE: *"I'm afraid of losing money when we sell. I don't want to lose our investment."*

So you are afraid *to lose*. Anything else?

ARLENE: *"Not that I can think of."*

Okay, let's look at Arlene's hopes and fears. Notice that they all contain verbs — action words. If there is no action, it is not a purchasing criterion.

HOPES	FEARS
• To cope	• To be safe
• To have another child	• To lose
• To make friends	
• To save	

SYLVIA: *"Why did you ask for fears as well as hopes?"*

To understand her motivations, I have to consider the full

spectrum of possibilities. She might express any motivation in either category. Arlene could hope to be safe instead of fearing danger. She could hope to profit instead of fearing loss. Arlene put two of her motivations in the negative category. However, you must convert them to positives, add them to her hopes, then eliminate any items that are redundant.

JOHN: *"Shouldn't we respect the painful connotation she placed on her fears?"*

If you do, when you speak of them you will remind her of their negative context. You want to build momentum by being as positive as you can. Don't you think Arlene would prefer an apartment in which she can hope to be safe and to profit rather than one in which she need not fear for her safety or risk losing her investment?

Purchasing Criteria
(Arlene's motivations for the purchase):
- To cope
- To have another child
- To make friends
- To save
- To be safe
- To profit

❧ LONG-TERM OBJECTIVES: THE BUYER'S LIFE GOALS

Long-term objectives are people's *Life Goals*, of which four are universal. In descending order of importance they are:
- SURVIVAL
- SECURITY — protection from harm.

- WEALTH ACCUMULATION — the flexibility to do things and have choices.
- SELF-ACTUALIZATION — the pursuit of personal interests and becoming the most you can be.

The more fundamental the life goal, the greater the sense of urgency. The first two are motivated by fear and avoiding pain. The second two are motivated by hope and the pleasure of accomplishment.

Arlene, why would you move to a new apartment?

ARLENE: *"To get something nicer."*

Why?

ARLENE: *"Because I could afford it, I guess."*

And if you couldn't afford it, why would you move?

ARLENE: *"Because I had to. Maybe I was being kicked out of my old apartment or I had a job transfer."*

Can anyone tell me what I just did?

SYLVIA: *"It seems to me that you went through two of the four life goals. The first answer was based on a hope to self-actualize with accumulated wealth, the second was based on fear of lost security."*

I'm glad you said "to me," because determining the category an answer fits into is a subjective judgment. Arlene must decide where the answer fits based on her own perception of reality.

JOHN: *"But how can you say that? Arlene's life isn't in jeopardy."*

It could be survival of a way of life. All the rungs on the *Life Goals Ladder* are subjective. I have seen salespeople to whom making a deal is life-threatening. They become so intense and anxious that they lose all perspective. They tend to do very well, but they leave a lot of "dead bodies" along the road. If it was a matter of survival, wouldn't you?

JOHN: *"Are you saying that whether something involves survival or security depends on a subjective sense of relative urgency?"*

Exactly. At the survival level, the urgency is most intense. As
you go up the ladder to security, and then to wealth accumulation, the urgency decreases and flexibility increases.
By wealth, I don't just mean money, but anything of value
that can be used later. Wealth can be information, friend-
ships, skills or whatever you value and want to possess.

JOHN: *"I guess someone seeking self-actualization would not
feel urgency but would enthusiastically pursue knowledge to
achieve his goal."*

Yes. So if you could buy an apartment from Donald Trump
or Sam Jones, who has just moved to California to start a
new job, with whom would you rather negotiate?

DIANE: *"Sam, because for him the sale is probably a security
issue. Donald Trump named his book* The Art of the Deal, *so to
him it's probably all self-actualization — the desire to be the
most he can be. Trump's drive to make a deal is a lot less urgent."*

Yes. Sam Jones has something to fear; Donald Trump has tri-
umphs to achieve. If Sam doesn't sell his apartment, he will
suffer. If Trump doesn't sell his apartment, he will be curious to find another way; it just becomes more interesting.

"I" Is for ISSUES

✐ UNDERSTANDING "I" FOR ISSUES

An issue is an obstacle blocking the road to your goal.

In $2 + X = 5$, X is an issue. To solve the equation, you must figure out
what X is. You identify X as 3 using deductive reasoning.

Say Mr. Leeds wants a three-bedroom apartment and is willing to
pay $1,000,000. You show him various apartments, and he decides to

buy one. Using deduction, you identified the missing variable, and the equation became complete.

In $X + Y = 10$, there are two issues: X and Y. You don't have enough information to figure out both variables, so the problem can be solved only by making an assumption. If you assume a value for one variable, you may have enough information to deduce the second.

Say that Joan Smith and Michael Gold decide to move to New York City and they want to buy an apartment. They are dealing with two variables: the first is convenience, coordinating all elements in making the move, and the second is finding the right home to fit their needs. If you show them the right apartment, and they don't buy, it is because you assumed that the first variable did not exist. To complete the equation, both variables must be resolved.

❀ THE ISSUES EQUATION

When you run into a snag, the key is to identify and test the variables in the equation leading to the sale. There are both direct and indirect issues.

Direct Issues are the elements of the Buyer's Formula, including the buyer's price, quality and utility requirements. You get this information expressly from the customer.

Indirect Issues may not be expressed but can still influence the sale. They include:

- PURCHASING CRITERIA: The underlying motivations for the purchase.
- PURPOSE: Is the buyer clear on why he is making this purchase?
- EMOTIONAL COMFORT: Is the buyer afraid to make this purchase?
- SOCIAL VALIDATION: Is the buyer wondering whether others will approve of this purchase?
- CONVENIENCE: Is the buyer wondering if it is the right time to buy?

When the variables are put together in an equation, it looks like this:

Issues Equation
Buyer Formula ✦ Purchasing Criteria ✦ Purpose
✦ Emotional Comfort ✦ Social Validation ✦ Convenience = Purchase

SYLVIA: *"How do I use this in dealing with a buyer?"*

Often, buyers don't tell you what's bothering them, or they may say that something is too expensive when the real problem is that they are afraid to make such a big commitment. When the obstacle is not clear, go through the elements of the *Issues Equation* with your customer. Make assumptions and deductions to identify the true obstacles blocking the sale.

SYLVIA: *"How do I figure out what is or isn't a problem?"*

Make a list of all the possible obstacles and go through it with your customer looking for clues. Go beyond his verbal statements, and use your gut responses to his answers as well as logic to get as much information as you can. If something doesn't feel right, keep probing.

❧ GETTING AT WHAT THE BUYER REALLY MEANS

When questioning your customer, don't accept glib or superficial responses. Probe for meaningful answers. Let me give you an example:

John, how are you today?

JOHN: *"Fine."*

In what way are you fine?

JOHN: *"I feel pretty good, and it's a nice day out."*

In what way do you feel pretty good?

JOHN: *"I don't have any pain, and I am alert."*

What kind of pain do you normally have?

JOHN: *"I have a bad back, and sometimes I have to work it out."*
    What's the problem you have to work out?
JOHN: *"It's an old football injury."*

    Notice that when I kept probing, John gave me increasingly rich information. At first he was superficial, but as I probed, his answers became more meaningful.

SYLVIA: *"When inquiring about issues, how much should you probe?"*

    As much as it takes until you learn what the buyer wants. You must get past his initial superficial response to figure out his rationale for making the purchase. Use your good sense and intuition. Does this response correlate with your other information? Does it form a logical framework leading toward the purchase? If answers are inconsistent, continue to probe for additional facts.

"W" Is for WHY

UNDERSTANDING "W" FOR WHY

If an obstacle is blocking the path to a sale, you must try to understand it. Not only what it is, but why it exists. Different types of issues must be dealt with differently.

    A *Substantive Issue* exists when some requirement in the customer's Buying Formula or Purchasing Criteria remains unsatisfied. You address this with additional information.

    A *Virtual Issue* appears when the customer is afraid to divulge the real problem, so he makes up an excuse for not buying. He may fear confrontation or be uncomfortable about describing the actual impediment to moving forward with the deal.

Say an apartment buyer repeatedly asks for a large space with lots of light at a specified cost. When shown exactly what he says he wants, he says he doesn't like the color of the marble in the lobby. If this was never part of the Buying Formula, your radar should go off immediately. Is this the real reason for not proceeding with the deal or just an excuse? You need to probe to find out.

A *Red Herring* is a false issue manufactured by the buyer to either delay or divert attention away from something he hopes you won't focus on.

Say a buyer likes an apartment and knows that if he doesn't make an immediate offer he will lose it, so he makes an offer that is accepted. However, when asked for the name of his attorney, he says he must find one and doesn't give the name until the salesperson calls a few days later. Then he "loses" the contract. Another contract is sent, and there is further delay. Finally, the buyer says he has changed his mind and has signed a contract on another property. He was dragging his feet to see if he could find a better deal before making a commitment.

A *Fundamental Issue* is a core position about which the buyer is inflexible. Trying to get him to adjust his thinking is like telling a family going into a car dealership for a minivan that they should buy a two-seater sports car. To the buyer, any effort to get him to change is so absurd as to create only anger. Attacking a fundamental issue will create greater animosity.

Say a couple is looking for a two-bedroom apartment because the wife is pregnant and they want a second bedroom for the child. After the broker shows them several apartments, all of which are too expensive, he takes them to see a large one-bedroom they can afford. He says: "I know you want a two-bedroom, but right now the market is too high. The price on this one-bedroom is fabulous. You can put your child in the living room temporarily, sell for a profit later and then purchase a two-bedroom."

This may be good advice, but if getting a two-bedroom is a fundamental issue for these buyers, the only thing the broker would succeed in doing is turning them off to working with him.

A *Strategic Issue* is raised by a customer for negotiating leverage to improve the terms of the deal.

Say that before closing on an apartment a couple notice that a 10% maintenance increase is not reflected in the contract. They tell their attorney: "Don't mention the error. We can use it at the closing to get a price concession for contract misrepresentation." The buyers are setting up a strategic issue to improve their negotiating position.

> JOHN: *"How do you deal with the nonsubstantive issues? What strategies should you use?"*
>
> When you suspect a Virtual or Red Herring Issue, you should go through the components of the Issues Equation and check each off the list. Talk to your buyer about each element. This may reveal the true problem.
>
> The best way to deal with a Fundamental Issue is to see it for what it is and accept it. If you have mistakenly attacked it, apologize. Don't try to get the buyer to reconsider. Say: "I made a mistake. I should have realized that this is a situation in which flexibility is inappropriate. Now I know better, and I am sorry." You must be sincere in your apology. After you redeem yourself, step back and figure out a new strategy.
>
> Look at a Strategic Issue as nothing more than an attempt to lessen the cost of the deal. Work through the details of the issues the customer has raised and affirm the value of what you are selling. A number of sophisticated real estate owners have told me that they always include at least one subtle point of controversy in each sales contract so that they have ammunition with which to defend themselves in case a Strategic Issue is raised.

"I" Is for INFORMATION

❧ UNDERSTANDING "I" FOR INFORMATION

People change their minds when they are given new information.

> Diane, do you recall the last time you made a mistake?
> DIANE: *"Sure. I recently offended a buyer by telling her that she needed to spend more money. As soon as I saw her response, I knew I made a mistake. She didn't want to be pushed, and she felt that I was pressuring her."*
> You didn't make a mistake. You made the best decision you could with the information you had. Only after the event did you get additional information that told you that what you said was inappropriate.

I believe that every decision you ever made was correct at the time you made it. You may have had inadequate information, but when you got more information you changed your mind. When someone acts, that action is right in the context of his knowledge at that time. Therefore, decisions can be information-impoverished but are never wrong.

> Say that you and I have to decide between eating at an Italian restaurant or a Chinese restaurant and that we like both cuisines equally. Which one should we go to?
> SYLVIA: *"I don't know enough to decide."*
> Let's say the Italian restaurant has an interesting menu, and the Chinese restaurant is a bit out of the way.
> SYLVIA: *"Then we should go to the Italian restaurant since it's more convenient."*
> But the Italian restaurant has been cited by the Health Department for violations.

SYLVIA: *"Now I'm turned off to the Italian restaurant. I don't want to go there anymore."*

Yes, and each decision you made was correct, from your point of view, until new information made you reassess. Before you knew the Italian restaurant was cited for health violations, it was a good choice. After you knew, it became a bad choice. It's not a function of right or wrong — it's a function of more or less information.

RELEVANCE AND MATERIALITY OF THE INFORMATION

Superfluous information never persuades a customer. Your points must be clear, direct and pertinent to have value.

Sylvia, what if the Italian restaurant's décor is red and the Chinese restaurant's is green?

SYLVIA: *"That doesn't matter to me."*

What if I said the Chinese restaurant was designed by a famous architect/designer and looks spectacular, while the Italian restaurant looks undistinguished?

SYLVIA: *"Then I would prefer to go to the dramatic designer restaurant."*

So it is not that décor is unimportant; it is the level of information that is important. When the information became richer, it became material.

If I were to say that there are 26 items on the Chinese menu and 28 items on the Italian menu, would that make a difference?

SYLVIA: *"No."*

What if I described specific menu items?

SYLVIA: *"That would be meaningful."*

In this example, the level of specificity increased the materiality. However, it could be the reverse: specific information could be immaterial and general information could be valuable. For example, a graph might show a general trend clearly, whereas the same information presented in more detail would be less clear.

> Does it matter that today is Wednesday?
> SYLVIA: *"Of course not."*
> It is irrelevant. To be useful, information must be meaningful and logically connected to the objective.

❧ THE QUALITY OF INFORMATION

When gathering information to present to your customer, keep in mind that there are different grades of information.

The highest grade is *Primary Information*, which comes from an objective verifiable source. Newspaper articles, prices and other information on comparable products and information from independent experts are examples of primary information. These sources have a high degree of credibility.

Secondary Information is your expert opinion based on your experience. It does not have the same credibility as primary information, although it may be just as accurate.

Tertiary Information is hearsay. For example, "I heard the building is going to be redoing the lobby" or "I've been told the vacant store up the street is going to become a gourmet-food emporium." There is no direct knowledge, only unverified rumor. This information is less credible than either Primary or Secondary Information.

Credibility does not depend only on the type of source but also its *Level of Authority*. If a newspaper says, "The price of New York City apartments is going up," that is Primary Information. However, the statement would have less Authority if made in *The Omaha Press* than in *The New York Times*.

You should always question the actual knowledge of the source. It is not uncommon for "experts" to create an aura of Authority without actually having expertise on the matter at hand. For example, attorneys sometimes advise buyers about apartment values even though they don't sell apartments; their aura of Authority gives their opinions more weight than their knowledge sometimes deserves.

A buyer asked me what a certain apartment was worth, and I said $250,000. Her salesperson said it was worth $300,000. She refused to pay that, asserting that the president of Bellmarc said it was worth less. The salesperson called me and convinced me that his valuation was more accurate than mine. Only when I told the buyer that I had changed my opinion did she agree to pay more. I had an aura of Authority that gave my valuation more weight, even though the salesperson worked in that neighborhood and knew more than me.

> **DIANE:** *"Is there anything else I should consider in gathering information?"*
>
> You want information the customer does not have. If he already knows something, telling it to him again is irrelevant. Remember, your purpose is to resolve issues that are obstructing your path. Keep your goals clearly in mind.

"N" Is for NEXT

✎ UNDERSTANDING "N" FOR NEXT

After you have identified your objective, the issues and the reasons those issues exist, and you have gathered your information, you should step back and think about what to do next: something or nothing.

DIANE: *"Why would I do nothing? Now that I'm prepared, shouldn't I use my knowledge to my advantage?"*

If you can find a response that gives you a high probability of success, then that is the way to go. However, if there is still a lot of uncertainty or a low probability of success, doing nothing may be better.

DIANE: *"But doing nothing doesn't get you anywhere."*

Not necessarily. New information is often revealed over time, and doing nothing does not mean that nothing will happen.

JOHN: *"But gaining control gives you an advantage."*

Yes, but if you play your cards, others will play theirs. If your hand is weak, you might want to pick up some new cards before initiating play. Waiting may bring new information, which creates new opportunities.

JOHN: *"But the other side may have a worse hand than you do."*

You have to weigh the probabilities and keep in mind who has the greater urgency. The more urgent the need, the more motivated the player will be to get the game going. The *Theory of Winners and Losers* holds that anyone with an advantage will want to maintain the status quo and do nothing, while a person with a weak position is motivated to act to alter the status quo.

Doing something or nothing should be an active choice, and you should think through the consequences either way. Analyze the possible results of inaction and consider how you would respond.

SYLVIA: *"What if you decide to act?"*

Then you should consider your alternatives. It's like a game of billiards: whatever you do is a stimulus — your action will cause a corresponding reaction. If your shot is clear and true, you should sink the ball in the pocket. If not, there will be a response, which you should try to predict before you hit the ball. Identify your course of action, consider the potential responses and be prepared for all possible outcomes. It is never preferable just to wait and see what happens; plan your responses.

JOHN: *"What if you want to take action, but you don't know what to do?"*

Then do anything. Whatever you do will elicit a response that will give you new information.

SYLVIA: *"But you could make things worse."*

Yes, but you might as well take your best shot. The resulting information may help you find a way to reach your goal. If doing nothing won't work, then anything else is better.

SYLVIA: *"But the buyer could get angry."*

Keep your options open for as long as possible. Things often don't go as you expect, and if you have left yourself no alternatives you risk getting stuck. Learn from the buyer's response so you can be more effective with your next action. My partner has a saying: "A good thief opens the rear door before he goes in the front."

Don't judge your buyer's response as good or bad — it just is. Getting stuck in anger and frustration will limit your choices. Step back. Look hard at your buyer's interest, not yours. He is looking out for himself, and it is proper for him to do so.

❧ SUMMARY

The key to success in sales is to have a selling strategy *"Only I WIN"* represents an effective technique.

ROBERT: *"What does 'Only I WIN' stand for?"*

O = OBJECTIVES. Be clear about what you want to achieve.

I = ISSUES. Identify the obstacles in the way of your goal.

W = WHY. Determine why the issues exist.

I = INFORMATION. Gather information to address the issues.

N = NEXT. Decide what your next move will be.

DONNA: *"What are the customer's different objectives?"*

SHORT-TERM OBJECTIVES: His *quality, utility* and *cost* specifications for this purchase (i.e., his *Buying Formula*).

MIDDLE-TERM OBJECTIVES: His motivation for making this purchase (i.e., his *Purchasing Criteria*).

LONG-TERM OBJECTIVES: *Life Goals*, which may determine his level of urgency and/or flexibility regarding this purchase.

JONATHAN: *"What is an issue?"*

An issue is an obstruction on the path to a sale.

CAROL: *"What is the* Issues Equation?*"*

The Issues Equation is shorthand for the common problems blocking a purchase. Probe your customer about each element in the equation to identify the obstacles in his way.

Issues Equation

Buyer Formula **+** Purchasing Criteria **+** Purpose
+ Emotional Comfort **+** Social Validation **+** Convenience **=** Purchase

RITA: *"What if the customer's answers are superficial?"*

If you keep asking for more specific information, the answers should become more meaningful.

SYLVIA: *"What are the different types of issues?"*

SUBSTANTIVE ISSUE: A problem that can be addressed with information.

VIRTUAL ISSUE: An excuse the customer makes up to hide the real issue, which he is reluctant to reveal.

RED HERRING: A false problem created to delay the deal or divert attention away from something.

FUNDAMENTAL ISSUE: A criterion so basic to the buyer that you risk offending him if you question it.

STRATEGIC ISSUE: An issue to gain leverage in negotiations.

JOHN: *"What is materiality and relevance?"*

The information you give your customer should always pertain to the purchase (relevance) and be significant enough to affect his decision (materiality).

DIANE: *"What are the different types of information?"*

PRIMARY INFORMATION: Information from independent sources, like newspapers or independent experts.

SECONDARY INFORMATION: Information from you based on your knowledge and experience.

TERTIARY INFORMATION: Unsubstantiated hearsay or rumor.

CAROL: *"What is an 'aura of Authority'?"*

At times experts in one field appear authoritative on subjects about which they have no special knowledge.

CASSANDRA: *"What do you do after gathering information?"*

Make a conscious decision to do something or nothing.

MICHAEL: *"What is the* Theory of Winners and Losers?"

In a controversy, the one with the strongest position will do nothing and seek to maintain the status quo. The one with a weaker position will want to take action.

MARY: *"What if you want to do something that will move the sale forward?"*

Think through the probability of success of each alternative and choose the one most likely to succeed. Plan what to do if your action backfires; always have alternatives in mind.

MICHAEL: *"What if you want to act but don't know what to do?"*

Do anything. Any action will generate a response that will give you new information.

❦

Keep Your Eye on Your Options

RAMSES WAS ONE OF THE MOST POWERFUL PHARAOHS IN EGYPT. HE BUILT MANY GREAT TEMPLES BUT WAS A CRUEL MASTER. ONE DAY, A SLAVE BROUGHT A DONKEY BEFORE HIM. RAMSES ASKED ANGRILY, "WHAT IS THE MEANING OF THIS?"

THE SLAVE FELL TO HIS KNEES, "OH, PHARAOH, I COME WITH BAD NEWS AND GREAT NEWS. A STONE FELL FROM THE SIDE OF THE NEW TEMPLE, AND IT WILL NOT BE READY ON TIME." THE PHARAOH WAS FURIOUS. "YOU WILL DIE FOR THIS!" HE SAID.

THE SLAVE MEEKLY SAID: "OH, YES, MY LORD, I UNDERSTAND. WOULD YOU LIKE TO HEAR THE GREAT NEWS?"

"SPEAK."

"PHARAOH, THE GREAT GOD OSIRIS CAME TO ME IN A DREAM AND TOLD ME HE WISHED TO MAKE YOU A GOD. HE SAID HE WOULD TEACH ME A SPECIAL LANGUAGE SO I COULD LEARN FROM THIS SACRED DONKEY HOW YOU MAY BECOME A GOD."

"OSIRIS WISHES TO MAKE ME A GOD? HOW SOON CAN YOU LEARN THIS LANGUAGE?"

"IT WILL TAKE ME FIVE YEARS, MY LORD."

"OKAY, YOU HAVE FIVE YEARS. IF AT THAT TIME YOU ARE UNABLE TO COMMUNICATE WITH THE DONKEY AND OSIRIS, YOU WILL DIE A HORRIBLE DEATH."

THE SLAVE THANKED HIM PROFUSELY AND LEFT.

HIS FRIEND WAS SHOCKED AT THE NEWS. "YOU FOOL," HE SAID. "YOU CAN'T TALK TO THAT DONKEY. YOU'RE DOOMED!"

THE SLAVE SAID: "FIVE YEARS IS A LONG TIME. THE PHARAOH MAY DIE, THE DONKEY MAY DIE, I MAY DIE — BUT TODAY I LIVE."

❦

CHAPTER 9

℘

Making an Effective Presentation

In addition to the content, the form in which you present information to the customer is important. The right structure can enhance his understanding of your message.

℘ THE BASIC REQUIREMENTS FOR AN EFFECTIVE PRESENTATION

To present the information you have gathered in the most effective way, it is essential to choose the right structure. Structure is how you organize information so that your message is a coherent whole. The information should lead clearly and logically to your desired outcome.

Any sales presentation (which can be a formal presentation or an informal series of discussions) must have *direction*: a beginning, middle and end. The beginning point is usually identifying the need to be fulfilled; the middle provides information addressing that need; and the end is the logical conclusion.

Each component of the sales presentation should have *meaning* and lead toward your objective. Superfluous elements distract from your argument and diminish the strength of your conclusion. A good presentation should answer questions or explore possibilities that directly address the buyer's underlying need.

A good sales presentation is *concise*. Even when a presentation's structure is logical and each item is relevant, too much information can diminish the overall impact. You need to distinguish critical arguments from those that are less crucial as well as from supporting information. Make sure your key points aren't obscured by extraneous material. A tree will be noticed more clearly in a field than in a forest.

The parts of the presentation should logically *correlate*. They should follow easily from one part to the next so the thought process doesn't get disjointed. There should be no inconsistencies or irrelevancies, and you should build logically toward your conclusion.

❧ STRUCTURAL FORMS

I have identified four structural forms for effectively presenting information. The first is a *Hierarchical Structure*. Here, you define an issue, then answer questions about it like "Who?" "What?" "When?" "Where?" "Why?" or "How?" Then you probe further for greater detail. The format looks like this:

Principle or Problem

Who? What? When? Where? Why? or How?

Who? What? When? Where? Why? or How? Specifically

Each ensuing step explores the same question or questions with greater specificity. You can also reverse the process by starting with the details and then asking, "What does this logically mean?" or "What should I logically do?" When you do this, the Hierarchical Structure flows from detail to a broader meaning.

The second format is a *Sequential Structure*. Here you review events chronologically to show cause-and-effect relationships that clarify a current problem. You can also enumerate steps (Reason 1, Reason 2, etc.) leading to your conclusion.

The third format is a *Statistical Structure*, in which alternatives are compared on the basis of concrete measurable criteria. For example, the square footage of various apartments can be compared to determine which have more or less space. Statistical Structures also include computational presentations. Values can be displayed in equations or tables that compute to a meaningful conclusion.

The fourth format is a *Visual Structure*, in which you create meaning by giving information in a sensory way. A metaphor or analogy would be an example of a visual structure. The story creates a mental picture, which you then logically connect to the purchasing decision. Visual Structures can also be explicit through the use of charts and graphs. The key is that some image or sensory association provides information that gives the customer a new perspective and greater clarity about the purchase.

> Okay, can anyone tell me when a Hierarchical Structure might be used?
>
> JOHN: *"When I am trying to find out what a customer wants, wouldn't I ask, 'Who, What, When, Where, Why or How?' and then probe further for specificity?"*
>
> Of course. This is the standard format you use for gathering information. However, in presenting information, we want to formulate a structure for communicating knowledge out to the customer rather than in to the salesperson.

An example of using this form of presentation would be a salesperson seeking to focus on the key elements of the product so that the buyer can focus on these criteria in analyzing his choices.

For example, I might define buying an apartment into specific criteria like location, building, light and space and then present information about these specific qualities for each apartment. By comparing these criteria among different alternatives, the buyer can more effectively and efficiently decide which apartment he likes because critical elements have been identified and quantified.

When would you use the Hierarchical Structure to go from specific details to broad principles?

MICHAEL: *"When the customer can't see the forest from the trees?"*

Yes. You would start by clarifying your own thinking. Sometimes the details involved in a complex sale can be confusing or overwhelming. Then you have to step away and look at the big picture. Once the big picture is clear to you, make it clear to your customer as well. When you focus on the main points, the details often fall into place or fade in importance.

Let's go to Sequential Structure. When would that be appropriate?

MARY: *"When I review apartments with a customer, I often say something like: 'First we saw an apartment with a big living room in a low-prestige building. Then we went to a nicer building, but the living room was smaller by two feet. The third apartment was in a really great building, but the living room was tiny. I discuss the apartments in the order we saw them and compare specific attributes. We can then generalize about market values and trade-offs in order to decide what to do."*

MICHAEL: *"I sometimes propose a time sequence to my buyer. I ask him to assume that he purchased the apartment, enjoyed living there, then sold it for a profit. I tell him that he can use the proceeds to purchase an even better apartment. I create a time line from the present to an appealing future."*

JONATHAN: *"Sometimes I count the reasons the buyer should make the purchase: Reason 1, Reason 2, Reason 3 and so on."*

These are all effective uses of Sequential Structure. Enumeration can also be in the form of instructions like, "First you do X, then Y, then Z."

When might you use a Statistical Structure?

JONATHAN: *"When I do computations to show a customer how he can qualify for a mortgage."*

Yes, any financial analysis that computes to a conclusion or any presentation in which variables are quantified then displayed in comparative form is a Statistical Structure. It also applies when you rate variables to compare them — for example, "How do you rate the products you have seen on a scale of 1 to 10?"

Can anyone give me an example of a Visual Structure?

JONATHAN: *"Any picture that clarifies the customer's thinking, like a pie chart or bar chart."*

Yes, graphs and charts clarify relationships and meaning and are Visual Structures, but so are analogies and metaphors. Say you want to address a problem indirectly; you can create a word picture to communicate your message.

You can construct metaphors by taking animals, inanimate objects or humans and pitting them against themselves or their environments. Put them in situations in which there is movement. Can you give me a problem a buyer might have?

SARA: *"He is afraid to make an offer."*

Let's use an animal's relationship to its environment.

If a leopard hesitates, it will not eat. Even if it runs hard, it may not catch its prey, but standing still guarantees that the leopard will go hungry. You will never buy an apartment unless you make an offer. The spoils go to those who are not afraid to act.

JONATHAN: *"How about losing a deal?"*

Let's take an inanimate object.

Water flowing downstream has obstacles in its path, but they stop it only momentarily; it builds up energy for the next opportunity to continue on. Nothing is lost; there is only a new direction to the flow. Losing a deal gives you more momentum and more knowledge. You've gone around the rocks, learned how to change your direction and are better prepared to continue on.

Test possible variations; you will find that ideas come naturally as you explore the possibilities. Create a stock of metaphors to use in recurring situations.

Metaphors and analogies are powerful teaching tools. They limit psychological resistance because the listener doesn't know the meaning until the story has been told and interpreted. The message is often received with less resistance than if you just stated your underlying idea. When you finish the metaphor, be sure to connect it to your specific situation. Make sure the buyer gets your point.

SARA: *"How do we use these presentation formats in selling?"*

Each of us has a natural strategy for processing information. Your strategy may be different from the buyer's. These structures allow you to present information in different ways, so you have choices. If you give a chronological presentation and your customer is resisting your ideas, try presenting the information in a metaphor or some other visual form. If that doesn't work, try a hierarchical presentation. Finding the most effective way to communicate your ideas to your buyer is an important part of being understood.

JOHN: *"Can you combine different forms of presentation?"*

Yes. You might first present your ideas in one way and then repeat the same ideas in another way. They may have a cumulative effect. The key is to consider all the possibilities to find the best way to get your idea across to your specific customer.

✐ SUMMARY

Having something important to say is meaningful only if the person receiving the information understands it. You must structure your presentation so that your information and ideas get through.

JOHN: *"What are the fundamental requirements for an effective presentation?"*

It should have direction: a beginning, middle and end. It should also be concise, the parts should correlate and each component should add meaning to the whole.

CASSANDRA: *"What is a* Hierarchical Structure?"

In a Hierarchical Structure, you take a problem and present increasingly specific information until the key components are clear. You can also reverse the process by starting with a series of disparate bits of information and finding the broader meaning from the detail.

RENE: *"What is a* Sequential Structure?"

Reviewing information chronologically or enumerating the reasons for doing something in a logical sequence, like 1, 2, 3 and so on. Sequential Structures are useful for gaining control over large quantities of data and for putting things in their proper context. They can also help you remind the buyer of things he might forget.

MICHAEL: *"What is a* Statistical Structure?*"*

Mathematical analysis using assigned values to compare things in a mathematical way. This is an efficient way to compare alternatives and create logical connections between seemingly disparate bits of information to heighten clarity.

ROBERT: *"What is a* Visual Structure?*"*

Anything that conveys information in a visual way. It can be a graph or a chart or a picture in words, like a metaphor or analogy. Word pictures are particularly effective in overcoming buyer resistance, since the message must be heard and interpreted before being understood.

KEN: *"How do you create a metaphor?"*

First be clear about what you are trying to communicate. Then place a human, animal or inanimate object in a situation that demonstrates your point. You can put your subject in conflict with others, the environment or himself, but the situation should have action. Finally, connect the story to your specific situation and the point you are making.

Neither Overdo It nor Be Indifferent.

ONCE AN ELDERLY KING CALLED ON HIS WISEST ADVISER FOR ADVICE ON WHICH OF HIS THREE SONS SHOULD INHERIT HIS THRONE. THE ADVISER PROPOSED THAT EACH SON BE GIVEN A SAPLING TO PLANT AND CARE FOR. THE FIRST SON CARED FOR HIS TREE DILIGENTLY. EVERY DAY HE WATERED IT, PULLED THE WEEDS AND FERTILIZED IT. THE SECOND SON PLANTED THE TREE AND WAS THEN INDIFFERENT TO IT. THE THIRD SON MONITORED HIS TREE FROM TIME TO TIME, WATERING IT AND GIVING IT ATTENTION AS HE SAW FIT.

A VIOLENT STORM CAME, AND THE FIRST TREE WAS QUICKLY UPROOTED. SINCE THE ELDEST SON HAD CARED FOR IT SO TENDERLY, ITS ROOTS HAD NO NEED TO GO DEEP INTO THE EARTH FOR NOURISHMENT. IT HAD NO FOUNDATION TO WITHSTAND THE STORM. THE SECOND TREE WAS ALSO QUICKLY UPROOTED. SINCE IT NEVER RECEIVED ANY CARE, IT HAD NO STRENGTH TO ENDURE HARDSHIP. THE THIRD TREE BENT TO THE WIND BUT STAYED FAST. BECAUSE IT HAD BEEN TENDED TO IN MODERATION, ITS ROOTS GREW DEEP INTO THE EARTH, AND IT GREW STRONG.

THE WISE ADVISER RECOMMENDED TO THE KING THAT THE THIRD SON INHERIT THE THRONE, AND SO IT WAS DONE.

CHAPTER 10

Understanding Different Points of View

You will gain greater understanding if you look at a problem from another perspective.

SEEING DIFFERENT POINTS OF VIEW

Alternative perspectives offer new possibilities for finding solutions to the obstacles in the way of a sale.

[Neil holds an empty coffee cup so that only the bottom is visible.]

If I look at this cup from this angle, it looks round and flat. To understand it better, I need to look at it from different perspectives.

[Neil shifts the cup's position.]

If I look at it from the side, or from above, I get more information. Likewise, there are different ways to view your buyers. Seeing them from different perspectives gives you new information that broadens your awareness.

> DIANE: *"What new information do you mean?"*
> Say I show you a picture of the Grand Canyon — does that give you the experience of being there?
> DIANE: *"Of course not. There is more to experience than can be pictured; there is the feeling of being there and having it all around you."*

You have two levels of awareness: one that you can express and another that is beyond words. The first is the smaller part of your awareness, your consciousness. The second and larger part is your subconscious. This is where the action is. Your subconscious stores the vast majority of your experiences and has a wealth of resources for solving problems. You can use the feelings, intuitions and awareness available there to help you sell.

Let's do an exercise. John, you be a seller asking $800,000. You believe this is reasonable and need this amount for your next home.

Diane, you be a buyer who has offered $600,000 and believes that John's home is worth about $700,000.

I want each of you to try to convince the other to accept your valuation. You should both be standing while you do this. Leave plenty of room, because a third person, Carol, is going to walk around both of you as you talk.

Carol, you are the Observer. Start by standing behind John. Listen, but don't try to put what you are learning into words. Once you have the information available from that position, stand behind Diane. Listen to the conversation from that perspective and get any information you can from being there. After you do this, go to the "triangular" position and listen from that point of view. Stand between the two of them, yet away, as if you were the third point in a triangle.

[As John and Diane speak, Carol first observes from behind John, then from behind Diane and, finally, from the triangular position. Then she looks at Neil.]

Carol, did you notice anything different by standing in the different locations?

CAROL: *"Absolutely. I became more attuned and sympathetic to each person and his or her arguments when I stepped behind him or her. By standing in the triangular position, to observe both, I became more aware of the dynamics between them. It was more holistic. I was taking it all in rather than taking sides."*

Is this information important?

CAROL: *"I have a much clearer sense of what is going on."*

Carol, now I want you to picture Diane and John having this conversation in your mind.

CAROL: *"Okay."*

See yourself floating up in the air and observe their conversation from above.

[Carol imagines observing the conversation from above. Then she looks at Neil.]

Now you have observed from four different viewpoints: behind each person, at the triangular position and above. What can you tell me about each?

CAROL: *"When I was behind each person, I felt more connected to his or her feelings. I was on his or her side. I also felt the strengths and weaknesses of each argument. At the triangular position, I took the conversation in without favoring either side. Going above was confusing. I felt like an angel looking down at them and judged the conversation differently."*

JOHN: *"This is weird. Being an angel is not my idea of getting new perspectives on a conversation."*

It's not right for you, yet this is a point of view that Carol created for herself, so for her it was appropriate.

SYLVIA: *"Which point of view is correct?"*

All of them. They are different perspectives on the same thing.

SYLVIA: *"If they are really the same thing, why go through this exercise?"*

Carol, you said you got additional information from each

perspective. Can you describe to us each point of view?

SYLVIA: *"No, not completely. I just have an additional insight."*

You can't tell us because a lot of it is subconscious; you don't have words to explain what you now know.

HOW TO MAKE AN EFFECTIVE DECISION

To be most effective, you should understand how to use each part of your mind as a resource. The Multi-Perspective Decision-Making Model should help you grasp the most effective method for problem-solving and decision-making.

The Multi-Perspective Decision-Making Model

THE LIBRARY: Imagine that you are in a Library with books on every wall from floor to ceiling categorized by subject.

You pick a book off a shelf and begin to read — it contains one of your experiences, with a clearly defined beginning, middle and end. Your mind has categorized this experience and placed it on this shelf. You open a second book; it is another of your experiences, also with a beginning, middle and end. In fact, each book on each shelf contains one of your life memories, and the Library as a whole is your accumulated life experience. The categories in the Library represent the way you group your memories.

THE READER: Who is reading these books of experience? You are. You are also evaluating new experience and placing it in the appropriate category and on a specific shelf. One way you may define memories is as pleasurable or painful, and you enjoy re-reading the books in some sections more than others. As you read, you feel all the emotions in the story. You become totally involved in the evolving event.

THE OBSERVER: Who is watching the Reader? You are. As the Observer, you do not read; instead, you see it all. The Observer knows the contents of the Library in general rather than specific terms and does not feel pain or pleasure in the stories. The Observer doesn't categorize experience but is aware that the Reader has done so. The Observer has a removed, holistic perspective.

THE HIGHER SELF: Your Higher Self is at the door of the Library and can see both what is in the room and beyond. While the Higher Self knows what both the Reader and the Observer are thinking, he can see beyond the Library to make evaluations of right and wrong.

⁂ UNDERSTANDING THE PEOPLE IN THE LIBRARY

The Reader is the part of you that is connected to specific past experiences and categorizes new experiences. The Observer is the part of you that is removed and able to consider things dispassionately and from a holistic perspective. The Higher Self is moral and spiritual. You must access all three perspectives to learn everything you can before deciding how to act.

Let me give you an example. After the tragic events at the World Trade Center in September 2001, my company's Internet site wasn't working properly, and the e-mail was inoperative. The head of the computer department told me that various companies provided Internet services, and we reviewed the available options. I became the Reader. After reviewing the information, I identified the best vendor. It was a more financially secure company and would provide more reliable service at no increase in cost. I then stepped into the role of Observer to consider the big picture: the Internet would be up, and the salespeople would be happy. I then went to my Higher Self and confronted a problem. I was abandoning a small vendor who was struggling to survive and doing his best to take care of his customers under difficult circumstances. Suddenly the decision to move no longer felt right. There might be another, more normal time when I could have made this decision, but my Higher Self would not let me do it then. I stayed with our original vendor and gave him a chance to get back on his feet.

ACCESSING THE BUYER'S PERSPECTIVE

When a buyer is engaged in a negotiation, he is so intimately connected to his point of view that it's as if he were in a trance.

> When you are reading, can you pay attention to anything else?
>
> **SYLVIA:** *"No, I need to concentrate. There may be background music or sound, but my attention is focused on my book."*
>
> When your buyer is concentrating on a book in his Library, he, too, becomes impervious to the information around him. To expand his frame of reference to include you, you must find a way of entering into his experience. You do this by validating what the buyer is reading. Affirmation will make the Reader extend the story to include you and what you have to say.
>
> You affirm your buyer's experience by using the methods

we have already discussed. Observe and affirm his beliefs, words, body language and patterns. Then you can move in one of two directions. You can expand the story by adding new details, or you can ask the Reader for permission to talk to the Observer by proposing that the buyer "step away" from his immediate concerns and explore the problem from a further perspective. You are asking the buyer's permission to disassociate from the emotional connection, and to look at the problem more dispassionately.

JOHN: *"Why do you have to ask permission from the Reader?"* Because the Reader is the gatekeeper to experience; only through the Reader can the buyer access the information in his Library.

CAROL: *"Why can't you just tell the buyer what you want to say?"* You can, but if he is reading one of the books in his Library of experience he may not hear you. Even if he does, he may not agree with you unless you conform to his beliefs.

CAROL: *"But if the buyer believes something that isn't true and you tell him the truth, won't he hear it?"* Maybe, maybe not. He has his own beliefs. If what you say does not fit his reality, he won't pay attention. You are *Shifting*: trying to impose your beliefs on the customer and insisting that he do things your way. Try *Switching*: step away from your perspective and enter that of the customer.

Say I go to the store to buy us dinner. I get filet mignon, potatoes, steak sauce and beer. Since I like this meal, I assume you will too. I am shifting my tastes onto you. However, you tell me that you are a vegetarian. If I want to make you happy, I should ask myself, "What should I buy to satisfy *you*?" If I switch from my own tastes to yours, I am far more likely to draw a correct conclusion.

❦ LEARNING TO UNDERSTAND

The purpose of switching is to become fully aware of the customer's perspective. To do a deal, you need to learn about your customer. The more information you gather from him, the fewer assumptions you will need to make, and the more you will be able to see things his way.

> CAROL: *"Isn't the most important thing to listen? If I listen to the buyer, he will tell me what I need to know to help him."*
> You have to go deeper than that. When your buyer speaks, you can hear, listen or understand. To *sell*, you need to understand. [Neil taps on the table.]
> You *heard* that, but it was just a noise without meaning.
> When you *listen*, you can repeat back what was said, but you haven't gotten its full meaning.
> When you *understand*, you are aware of the full meaning of what was said. You have processed it on both the conscious and subconscious levels.
> How many times has someone clearly not gotten what you said even though he could repeat it word for word? He may have listened, but he didn't understand. Salespeople who are frustrated with their customers often say, "They don't listen!" Not true. They are listening; they just don't understand. Your job is to explore why.
> SYLVIA: *"Maybe the customer doesn't want to understand."*
> True. But maybe you haven't given him a foundation for the new information, so it is too disjointed. Say I was reading a biography of George Washington and found a page in the middle about John F. Kennedy. I wouldn't understand how it fits. I might read it, but it wouldn't help me understand the story I was reading.

❧ UNDERSTANDING CONSCIOUS AND SUBCONSCIOUS AWARENESS

The customer may also be so busy planning what he is going to say next that your incoming data is blocked because his brain is fully utilized.

JOHN: *"What do you mean?"*

John, did you ever have a problem you could not solve, but after leaving it for a while you found you could solve it?

JOHN: *"Sure, many times."*

And when you left it alone, did you churn the problem in your head? Did you try to work it through?

JOHN: *"Sometimes, but often I worked on something else and then came back to it."*

Why do you think the answer came to you the second time around?

JOHN: *"I don't know."*

It was because your subconscious was working on it even while you did something else. Through this subliminal process you gained new insights and found solutions.

When you worry, do you do so intensely?

JOHN: *"Sometimes."*

When you are seriously worrying about a problem, you are thinking about it even when you are also thinking other things.

Say your wife just called and told you that your father had a heart attack and was in intensive care. She also said not to come to the hospital since there was nothing to do. She said to stay in class and that she would call you as soon as she knew something. Now here you are. If I were to say, "The weather is getting cold, isn't it?" how would you respond?

JOHN: *"I would be distant. I would say yes, but I would be thinking about something else."*

Exactly. Even as you said yes, your conscious mind would be wondering when your wife would call and hoping your father was all right. Your subconscious would be flooding your body with feelings of anxiety. So there are three components to your thinking: your external behavior, your consciousness and your subconscious.

John, would you be able to have a detailed discussion with me about the class material?

JOHN: *"No. I would be distracted by my thoughts and my feelings about my father. I couldn't concentrate on both things."*

At any given time, your mind can expend only a certain amount of energy. People who spend too much energy on external behavior limit their ability to process information consciously and/or subconsciously. If you are stuck, be sure to give yourself some downtime to let your subconscious work on the problem.

In addition to the application of energy, there is also a biological limitation on your ability to handle information. The brain can process only between five and nine bits of information at one time. If it has reached its full processing capacity, no new information can be absorbed.

SYLVIA: *"How do you know when this is happening?"*

A person who answers you very quickly is thinking about his reply while you are still talking rather than using his energy to understand your information. You can often tell when such buyers stop comprehending by watching their eyes. They defocus, or look up or down. If you see this, you know they are no longer processing what you are saying. The same is true when buyers are intense or speaking loudly. They have become so connected to their own stories that they are unable to absorb new information coming in.

SYLVIA: *"What can you do?"*

First you must understand what is happening. Energy is being diverted away from the subconscious to be used for the conscious and external behavior, preventing effective decision-making. The key is to direct the buyer's energy away from the overenergized areas.

One strategy is to pause after the buyer finishes speaking to slow down the pace. This permits broader application of the energy to other areas. You might say: "Hmmm, that's an interesting idea. I need a moment to think about it." Then, "I think your point has merit, and yet I would like you to consider another point of view as well." Finally, look at the buyer and ask, "Does my point make sense to you?" or "Do you understand what I'm saying?" This gets him to focus his energy on processing the new data.

If you can do it tactfully, it can also be very effective to get the buyer to repeat what you just said in his own words. Another strategy is to say, "Let's step back and think about this for a moment," or you can ask an open-ended question like, "If this occurs, then what will happen?" If you can get the buyer to become more passive and less verbal, then energy will be redirected to the subconscious for a more thoughtful reflection of new ideas.

JOHN: *"Would this apply when the buyer is angry or upset?"*

Sometimes, but when someone is angry or upset he is defending a closely held belief, and he is intensely focused. You must validate his idea and his concern before initiating any effort to explore another point of view. If you can't do this, create pauses in the conversation so that the intense energy can dissipate. Only then can you attempt to proceed constructively .

Remember to follow this advice yourself. If you feel yourself speeding up or getting too intense, slow down and let your energy apply to all your mental components.

ℳ SUMMARY

You can succeed in selling if you understand the purchase from your customer's point of view. You must consider his perspective every way you can, both consciously and subconsciously. Finally, you should consider why he might not be understanding your point of view.

MICHAEL: *"What are the four points of view for mentally observing a conversation?"*

POINT 1: Behind the seller.

POINT 2: Behind the buyer.

POINT 3: Between the buyer and seller forming a triangle with them.

POINT 4: Above the parties.

If you imagine listening to the parties from these four positions, you will get different information from each perspective. This will help you understand each point of view and be persuasive.

JOHN: *"What must you do to make an effective decision?"*

You must use all your resources to evaluate information. This includes using all three perspectives from the Multi-Perspective Decision-Making Model: the Reader, to reference your knowledge and past experience; the Observer, to look at the broader picture; and your Higher Self, to make a moral evaluation.

SUSAN: *"Why might your buyer not understand you?"*

He may lack the foundation of knowledge necessary to

understand the new material you are giving him, or he may see your information as conflicting with his values and beliefs. If so, you must affirm your acceptance of him and his ideas before he will entertain your ideas.

SARAH: *"What do you do after affirming the customer and his ideas?"*

You can either expand upon his experience by adding new information or you can ask him to step back and consider a holistic approach to the problem.

JOAN: *"What is* Shifting *vs.* Switching?"

In Shifting, you are projecting your own ideas onto the buyer and assuming that he wants what you want. In Switching, you are mentally stepping out of yourself and pretending to step into the buyer, thereby assuming his point of view.

CAROL: *"What is the difference between conscious and subconscious processing?"*

Your conscious mind evaluates information logically, in terms of cause and effect. Your subconscious has greater resources and processing capabilities, but it works subliminally — giving you information in the form of feelings, intuition and awareness rather than just logic.

CASSANDRA: *"Why is listening not enough?"*

You must go beyond listening to understand your customer's underlying motivations. You must comprehend his message on both the conscious and subconscious levels.

RITA: *"How much information can you absorb at any one time?"*

You can absorb just five to nine bits of information at any given time; this is a biological limit. If the limit is exceeded, critical information can be lost. If your buyer is thinking about something else, he won't be able to focus on your information.

CAROL: *"What does it mean if your buyer answers quickly? What can you do about it?"*

If someone answers quickly, that means he was preparing his answer while you were still talking. Once he has started preparing his reply, he is no longer focusing on what you are saying. You should try to get him to slow down and focus by pausing before you speak. Also, try to get him to acknowledge what you have said after each new piece of information. Another way to slow him down might be to say, "Let's step back and think about this for a moment." Don't present your information until the buyer is ready to focus on it.

☙

Even the Truth Is a Point of View

A CRIMINAL TRIAL ATTORNEY WAS SPEAKING TO A GROUP OF YOUNG STUDENTS. HE DESCRIBED HOW A MAN WAS ASSAULTED IN FRONT OF A GROUP OF PEOPLE. WHEN THE CASE WENT TO TRIAL, BOTH THE PROSECUTOR AND THE DEFENSE ATTORNEY PRESENTED WITNESSES.

THE PROSECUTOR'S WITNESS DESCRIBED HOW THE DEFENDANT, HIS FACE RED WITH RAGE, SHOOK HIS FIST AT THE VICTIM. HE SAW THE DEFENDANT'S ARM SWEEP WIDE, HITTING THE VICTIM ON THE JAW.

THE DEFENSE ATTORNEY'S WITNESS SWORE THAT THE VICTIM POINTED AT THE DEFENDANT AND PUSHED HIM IN THE CHEST. THE DEFENDANT LIFTED HIS ARM TO BLOCK THE VICTIM. HIS FACE TURNED RED, BUT HE WAS SWINGING ONLY TO BLOCK THE VICTIM'S IMPENDING BLOW.

THE TRIAL ATTORNEY ASKED THE CLASS WHOM THEY BELIEVED, AND ONE STUDENT ANSWERED THAT HE BELIEVED THE DEFENDANT WAS GUILTY OF ASSAULT. THEN THE ATTORNEY SAID, "THE VICTIM HAS THREE PRIOR CONVICTIONS, INCLUDING PHYSICAL ASSAULT." THE STUDENT SAID: "OH, THAT'S DIFFERENT. THE VICTIM MUST BE RESPONSIBLE." THE ATTORNEY SAID: "I MADE A MISTAKE. IT WAS THE DEFENDANT, NOT THE VICTIM, WHO HAD THE PRIOR CONVICTIONS." THE STUDENT WENT BACK TO HIS ORIGINAL OPINION.

THE ATTORNEY SAID: "YOU SEE HOW IT WORKS? YOU JUDGED WHAT HAPPENED WITHOUT EVEN BEING THERE! CAN YOU IMAGINE WHAT JUDGMENTS YOU WOULD HAVE MADE HAD YOU OBSERVED THE FIGHT? DON'T YOU THINK YOUR JUDGMENTS COLOR WHAT YOU SEE? SURE THEY DO. THAT'S WHY WE HAVE

TRIALS, BECAUSE EVERYONE HAS A DIFFERENT POINT OF VIEW, AND EACH PERSON SWEARS THAT HIS POSITION IS THE TRUTH. OF COURSE, TO HIM IT IS."

CHAPTER 11

ℯ𝒴

Persuasion

People change their minds on the basis of new information, which can come in three forms: new facts, a different perspective on existing facts or information enhancing the product's psychological appeal. You are most persuasive when you use all three in an overall strategy.

ℯ𝒴𝒐 TYPES OF INFORMATION

If a buyer is refusing to make a purchase, that decision is correct to him at that time. However, additional information may get him to change his mind. Information comes in three forms: *Substantive Information*, or new facts; *Reframed Information*, or a different perspective on existing facts; and *Psychological Information*, or information that enhances the product's emotional appeal. Since Substantive Information has already been discussed, I will now discuss the other two.

ℯ𝒴𝒐 REFRAMING INFORMATION

The frame is the label we put on something. It can imply "valuable" or "inexpensive," it can be "right" or "wrong."

> There are two pictures on the classroom walls. One is an oil painting of New York City with an ornate gold frame, and

the other is a watercolor with creative intermeshing shapes and a simple chrome frame.

Which painting do you think is more valuable?

JOHN: *"The one of New York City."*

Does anyone think the other painting is more valuable?

[No hands are raised.]

The painting of New York City was bought at a local frame store for $250. The watercolor was bought directly from the artist and is worth approximately $10,000. Why do you think you were all wrong?

DONNA: *"The oil painting just looked more expensive."*

What if I switched the frames? Say the ornamental gold frame was on the watercolor and the simple chrome frame was on the cityscape. Would that matter?

RITA: *"Definitely. One naturally assumes that the better painting will get the better frame."*

Consider this: Look at the watercolor; reframing it could alter its meaning without changing a brushstroke.

Statements are word pictures; when you give a statement a new label or context, a new meaning is revealed.

REFRAMING IN ACTION

Everything is neutral until you label it as good or bad. Its meaning can be changed by switching to another label.

Once I saw a salesperson crying; her mother was dying of cancer. She told me how painful it was to watch her mother whither away day after day. I asked if she had told her mother that she loved her; she said she had.

I said: "I know this is painful, and yet it is a gift that in her last hours you are able to show her your love and tell her how you feel. She will die knowing that you will always remember her and that your love for her was strong and heartfelt to the end. How often is it that only after someone has died do we reflect on what we wish we had said? We are so sorry that we never told him or her how we felt. You told your mother that you loved her while she was able to hear you. She will remember it forever, and so will you. Even more important is the love you are feeling right now and the pride your mother must feel in a daughter with the caring and the courage to comfort her at the end. What more could a mother hope for?"

You were all quiet as I told this story. You may feel sad, and yet you sense that there is another meaning. The story is positive because it has been labeled that way — by her, by me and by you.

Here's another example of reframing: of changing a negative into a positive. Think about a time something was terribly wrong and you were deeply hurt. It could have been an argument with someone important or a painful event. Picture that experience in your mind.

While looking at the picture, see it from your present perspective as part of the time line of your life. You are here today and it is in the past, where you can observe and analyze it. It was a challenge you met, overcame and learned from. It gave you new insights and made you stronger. Even though there was pain, you can now see the wisdom and strength that grew from that seed.

ఇ EXAMPLES OF REFRAMING

Developing positive responses to negative statements can motivate a change in position.

Give me some examples of negative statements to reframe.

ROBERT: *"I never have any luck!"*

It's wonderful that you never have any luck, because you have earned everything through hard work! Since you can't rely on chance, you had to learn skills. You control your destiny and your success.

SARA: *"I'm afraid to buy the apartment."*

I understand that you are afraid to buy the apartment; this is an important decision. It is wise to be afraid, because it matters. Now that you know it is good to be afraid, you will also know that it isn't fear, it's caution, that is the underpinning of your wisdom.

JOHN: *"I don't like the buyer."*

Isn't it wonderful that you don't like the buyer! I'm sure you're excited about making money off someone you don't like.

CAROL: *"The apartment is too small."*

Isn't it wonderful that the apartment is too small — if it were bigger, it would be too expensive, and you wouldn't be able to afford it. Because it is small, we might be able to get a really good deal!

SYLVIA: *"I feel like a failure."*

I know you feel like a failure, yet isn't failure the key to success? How can you move up in life without the courage to try new things? Your failures mean that you are taking risks instead of settling for the safe or easy way. You can't succeed in life unless you have failed first.

JOHN: *"I can't find an apartment I like."*

I understand that you can't find an apartment you like, yet isn't this because you are a careful buyer? You are insisting on the right apartment to suit your needs. I think it's wonderful that you are so clear about what you want. Obviously, when you find the right apartment you will be committed to buying it.

❦ STRATEGIES FOR REFRAMING

The strategy of Reframing is to look for another interpretation of a given statement. What techniques did you identify in my responses to the previous statements?

> SYLVIA: *"The first thing you did was repeat the statement you were going to Reframe."*
>
> When I restate what you said, I connect to it. You said it — you are connected to it. Now I must connect to it in order to understand it from a different point of view and give it a different label. The repetition also gives me time to think about my response.

> JOHN: *"How do you formulate the Reframes?"*
>
> There are two primary ways. The first is to emphasize the positive by saying, "Isn't it wonderful," restate the statement, then add "because" before the Reframe.
>
> The second, which I refer to as "You're right and yet," validates the speaker's position, then looks at it from a different perspective. You don't actually have to say "and yet," but you must connect the first statement to the Reframed point of view.

> CAROL: *"How do you think of what to say?"*
>
> It is as easy to create a positive label for something as a negative one. You choose a label by habit, and you can easily change your viewpoint.
>
> It may help to see the statement as an object. Picture it in tangible form in your mind, then imagine changing its position. Once you have moved it, ask your subconscious, "What is the meaning now?" By creating a mental picture, you are directly communicating with your subconscious — it will respond.

You can also consider the statement in the context of one of the patterns of behavior [*Chapter 4*]. For example, if the negative statement looks to the past, you can put a positive label on the future. If the customer says, "I have never been able to do this," you can say: "You're right! You have never been able to do this because you didn't know how. Now you have the information you need to go forward. I'm excited for you!"

If the negative is in the future, you can put a positive label on the past. If the customer says, "I'm afraid about what will happen," you can say: "Yes, you are afraid about what might happen. However, for every new experience there was a first time. You tried new things, you learned and you became wiser and more confident. This is like every other first time. You were rewarded for your courage then, and you will be rewarded now as well."

Good Reframing is an art. The key is to remember that everything is neutral until we attach a positive or negative label. It is useful to prepare a store of Reframes of buyers' common negative statements. Create a basic library of Reframes to use over and over again.

CAROL: *"How do you use Reframing in selling?"*

People will rethink their conclusions if given additional information. A Reframe gives a new perspective, which is new information. Identify the customer's reservations and formulate Reframes to convert the negatives to positives.

UNDERSTANDING ELEMENTS OF FORCE

Underlying all efforts of persuasion is the application of some force applied against a given position.

John, could you give me your pen please?

[John hands his pen to Neil.]

Now, how are you going to get it back?

JOHN: *"I'll ask for it."*

But what if I won't give it back so easily? What is the basis of your claim?

JOHN: *"You took it, and it's not yours."*

You are relying on my sense of fairness. You are asking me to feel guilt because there was no quid pro quo.

JOHN: *"I never thought of it that way, but I do want you to feel guilty that you are doing something wrong."*

You are using guilt to try to motivate me. This is *Psychological Force*.

Now let's say I believe I am entitled to the pen as payment for teaching you.

JOHN: *"Well, no one else will agree with that. You didn't take anyone else's pen."*

So I should give the pen back so that other people don't think ill of me. This is *Social Force*.

You could also use *Physical Force* to take it back or *Economic Force* to take something of value from me. These are the four forces: *Psychological, Social, Physical* and *Economic*.

To persuade, you must engage at least one element of force in some way. However, you could use positive rather than negative force. You could seek to persuade by arguing that something is fair and reasonable, socially enhancing, profitable or conducive to improved health and well-being. Whether you use positive or negative force, your objective is to motivate the customer to change. The key is to do it artistically, by identifying new Substantive Information and Reframed Information and by making your proposal psychologically appealing.

THE ART OF SELLING: A Scientific Approach

ℳ UNDERSTANDING PSYCHOLOGICAL YEARNING

Beyond reexamination of the facts is our desire to stay connected to our unique values and beliefs.

[Neil puts his right hand out toward John, who shakes it.]
Did anyone notice what just happened?

RICHARD: *"Yes, John shook your hand."*

John, I didn't tell you to shake my hand. Why did you do it?

JOHN: *"I just knew I was supposed to. It's what people do."*

[Neil places a $10 bill in front of Carol.]
Carol, what are you thinking?

CAROL: *"I'm thinking, 'What do you want?'"*

Since I gave you something of value, you assume you must reciprocate?

CAROL: *"Yes, I am wondering if what you ask me to do will be worth it or not."*

You are already focusing on whether the trade will be fair; you assume that reciprocity must occur — a quid pro quo.

CAROL: *"Absolutely."*

Your behaviors are governed by rules and assumptions so basic that they have become part of your personality. You want to conform to these rules — this is how you feel most comfortable. The universal desire to conform to certain rules can be used to persuade.

JOHN: *"Isn't that manipulation?"*

Yes, but anything you say that changes the buyer's mind is manipulation. It is your job to manipulate the buyer in an honest way to complete the sale.

John, how would you respond to these requests: First, "John, get me a pen." Second, "John, would you do me a personal favor and get me a pen?"

JOHN: *"I would respond to the second request before the first."*

But the content is the same, isn't it?

JOHN: *"Yes, but the second request was polite, and I felt more inclined to respond."*

You interpreted my expression of affinity as courtesy and were motivated to respond. Affinity, an expression of personal relationship, is a very effective persuasive technique.

The Basic Psychological Principles of Persuasion

There are seven fundamental persuasive techniques using psychological information that can get your buyer to change his mind about a purchase. The acronym A CARESS will help you remember them.

"A" IS FOR AUTHORITY. Information from a source perceived as authoritative can be very influential. We all seek advice from authorities. We go to doctors, lawyers and accountants, read newspapers and magazines and take directions from managers and employers. Since we see these people as knowing more than we do, we tend to accept their points of view. However, people often exaggerate the expertise of people they respect and ask their advice on subjects outside their areas of competence. Someone's actual Authority on one subject can give him an "aura of Authority" on many others.

Say a buyer likes a home but is afraid it may be overpriced. The sales agent says firmly: "I have been selling in this area for 15 years and know market values better than anyone. You should buy this apartment!" The buyer is convinced of the sales agent's Authority, so he decides to rely on her advice.

"C" IS FOR CONSISTENCY. Once a buyer has set his course, it is easy for him to become further committed to it, making change problematic.

Say a buyer keeps saying he wants a view and complains about the view in one apartment after another. Finally, the salesperson shows him an apartment with spectacular views. It is smaller and more expensive than the buyer desires, but the salesperson says: "You told me over and over that you want a view. This apartment gives you just what you want: a magnificent view. Don't miss your chance to get what you really want!" The salesperson is using Consistency to motivate the buyer.

"A" IS FOR AFFINITY. We are influenced by people with whom we have personal relationships or whose ideas we understand and relate to. You can use your connection with a buyer to influence his decisions. You might say, "Would you do this as a personal favor?" or "I know you, and this would be a good decision for you."

Say a couple with two young children are wondering if they should purchase an apartment. The salesperson says: "You know, my husband and I have children about the same ages as yours. We live in this neighborhood, and when we first moved we didn't know anyone either. We had to learn our way around, and our kids had to get used to a new school. It was tough, but I'm glad we did it; this is a nice neighborhood. It's hard to change, but I did it and you can too." The salesperson is trying to instill the sense that she shares the customer's concerns and interests; she is using Affinity to influence the buyers' decision.

"R" IS FOR RECIPROCITY. If someone perceives an exchange to be unfair, then a yearning for fairness will make him want to bring things back into equilibrium.

Say a seller wants $650,000, and the buyer will pay only $600,000. The salesperson tells the seller: "Both you and the buyer are reasonable people, and you both have legitimate points supporting your positions. Why don't you meet halfway? If you come down $25,000, I think the buyer will come up $25,000, and you will both have a fair deal." The salesperson is using Reciprocity to influence the seller.

"E" IS FOR EXCLUSIVITY. We want what others desire. When we acquire what others want, we have won a battle in a lifelong psychological war. Purchasing something that is "exclusive" is a validation of one's worth relative to other people.

Say a buyer wants a one-bedroom apartment. She sees many, but none are large enough. The salesperson says: "You know, I just received a listing at Trump Plaza for a one-bedroom. I know it is not as big as you want, but, think of it, you could afford to live in Trump Plaza! That's pretty amazing." The salesperson is using the lure of exclusivity to persuade the buyer to take a smaller apartment.

"S" IS FOR SCARCITY. When a product's supply is perceived as small, demand becomes high. As the supply diminishes, the buyer's psychological yearning for it increases.

For example, say a buyer asks the sales agent for a newly constructed building about buying a two-bedroom apartment. The sales agent says: "I'm sorry, we don't have any more two-bedrooms — they sold out really fast. If you want, I'll take your name in case one of the deals falls through." The buyer leaves his name and telephone number.

That evening, the sales agent calls the buyer and tells him a great two-bedroom just became available because the original buyer didn't qualify for financing. She says, however, that if he wants the apartment he has to tell her now. There is a list of potential buyers, and she will make another call unless he is ready to proceed. The buyer, not wanting to lose this opportunity, agrees to buy. He is motivated by Scarcity.

"S" IS FOR SOCIAL PROOF. This is what others will think about the purchase. Consciously or subconsciously, we all care what others think, and this motivates our decisions. You might say, "I know your friends will like it" or "Everyone will approve."

Say a buyer is unsure about purchasing an apartment, and the broker says: "I know you love to entertain. Can you imagine what your friends will say when they see this place? They will be so impressed!" The salesperson is using Social Proof to influence the buyer.

USING PERSUASIVE TECHNIQUES

Which of these techniques you use depends upon the situation. You can choose one, or several, to persuade a buyer.

> DIANE: *"What do you do after you select a technique?"*
> You can use it once or throughout your entire argument. Repetition in different words and contexts can be effective. You can also use several different persuasive techniques with the customer. Cumulatively, they can have a profound impact.
>
> I think of these techniques as seasoning on meat. Say I serve you plain chicken; it is rather bland until I season it to your taste. There is no change in the meat, only in the taste, but your desire to eat it increases radically. Using the acronym *A CARESS* improves the taste of the deal.

SUMMARY

To persuade your buyer to change his mind, you must identify the arguments behind his position and provide him with new information so that he will reconsider.

> KEN: *"What are the different forms of information?"*
> SUBSTANTIVE INFORMATION, or new facts.
> REFRAMED INFORMATION, or a new perspective on existing facts.

PSYCHOLOGICAL INFORMATION, or information that makes the product more psychologically desirable.

RITA: *"What does it mean to Reframe information?"*

You change the context in which it is considered. What was once "bad" can now be seen as "good."

CASSANDRA: *"What do you mean when you say that no experience is bad?"*

You have a given set of facts; which label you put on them depends on your perception at the time. A negative experience can be reframed and seen from a positive perspective.

JOHN: *"What are the elements of force?"*

PHYSICAL FORCE: People can be motivated by the prospect of physical benefit/harm.

ECONOMIC FORCE: People can be motivated by the prospect of economic profit/loss.

PSYCHOLOGICAL FORCE: People can be motivated through fairness/guilt.

SOCIAL FORCE: People can be motivated by social validation/social criticism.

To persuade, you must engage at least one element of force, either positive or negative.

DONNA: *"What are the seven persuasive techniques using psychological information?"*

I use the acronym A CARESS for the seven persuasive techniques:

AUTHORITY: The perception that someone has knowledge or stature makes the buyer more likely to follow his advice.

CONSISTENCY: The buyer will want to stick with a plan conforming to his values and beliefs.

AFFINITY: A buyer can be influenced by a salesperson with whom he has a personal relationship or a sense of commonality.

RECIPROCITY: People want and expect a deal to be fair. If they get something of value, they are willing to give value in return.

EXCLUSIVITY: The inability to have something makes you want it all the more.

SCARCITY: When something is perceived as scarce, the buyer's desire for it increases.

SOCIAL PROOF: The buyer will want to act in a way that will get others' approval.

❄❄

Loving to Sell and Selling to Love
Have a Lot in Common

I RECENTLY INTERVIEWED TWO ACCOMPLISHED PEOPLE: JOHN CASANOVA, A DESCENDENT OF THE LEGENDARY LOVER CASANOVA, WHO HAS TAKEN THE SKILLS PASSED DOWN FROM HIS GREAT-GREAT-GRANDFATHER AND APPLIES THEM TODAY, AND JOAN CASANOVA, JOHN'S SISTER, WHO IS ALSO SAVVY IN THE ARTS OF ROMANCE.

THEIR INSIGHTS HAVE APPLICATION TO THE ART OF SELLING. I HOPE THEY GIVE YOU FOOD FOR THOUGHT.

John Casanova on "Meeting a Beautiful Woman" and Joan Casanova on "Deciding on a Man"

JOHN CASANOVA

"WHEN I GO OUT FOR THE NIGHT, I ALWAYS DRESS TO FIT IN, AND I ALWAYS LOOK CLEAN AND ORDERLY. SOME PEOPLE REALLY GO FOR LOOKING DIFFERENT. NOT ME. I WANT TO MEET SOMEONE AND CREATE A CONNECTION, AND I INCREASE MY ODDS BY FITTING IN AND LOOKING NEAT."

SELLING STRATEGY: LOOK LIKE A PROFESSIONAL. BE "ORDERED" WHEN YOU MEET A CUSTOMER. CLOTHES THAT ATTRACT ATTENTION MAY BE SENDING A MESSAGE THAT DECREASES YOUR CHANCES OF MAKING THE SALE.

"IF I WANT TO CONNECT WITH A WOMAN, I NEED TO KNOW WHY SHE'S THERE. A WOMAN SELDOM COMES TO A NIGHTCLUB TO DRINK ALONE OR TALK TO FRIENDS. I PRESUME THAT SHE

WANTS TO MEET A MAN, BUT I DON'T TAKE IT FOR GRANTED."

SELLING STRATEGY: FIND OUT WHAT THE BUYER WANTS AS QUICKLY AND COMPLETELY AS YOU CAN. DON'T ASSUME THE ANSWERS; ASK THE QUESTIONS.

"MEETING A WOMAN IS LIKE GOING TO A CASINO: YOU PLACE YOUR BET AND HOPE FOR THE BEST. IF YOU DON'T PUT DOWN ANY MONEY, YOU'RE NOT GOING TO HAVE A GOOD TIME. GO AHEAD! GIVE IT A SHOT AND HOPE YOU GET A GOOD RETURN."

SELLING STRATEGY: BE READY TO TAKE A LOT OF LOSSES BEFORE YOU SCORE A WIN. SOMETIMES YOU WIN; SOMETIMES YOU LOSE. THE IDEA IS TO ENJOY THE WHOLE PROCESS.

"I NEVER GO OUT LOOKING FOR THE PERFECT WOMEN. I GO TO HAVE A GOOD TIME, AND DO IT SINCERELY. IF I MEET SOMEONE SPECIAL, I FIND OUT AS MUCH ABOUT HER AS I CAN. I PROBE FOR HER INTERESTS AND LET HER DO THE TALKING. IF SHE ASKS ABOUT ME, I TELL HER STORIES. STORIES ARE A LOT MORE FUN THAN FACTS OR BRAGGING. THE BEST STORIES ARE FUNNY ONES IN WHICH I GOT THE SHORT END OF THE STICK."

SELLING STRATEGY: EVERY NEW CUSTOMER IS AN OPPORTUNI-TY. NEVER DECIDE THAT ANY SALE IS "NOT WORTH IT." WHEN YOU HAVE AN INTERESTED BUYER, ASK A LOT OF QUESTIONS AND GET ALL THE INFORMATION YOU CAN. IF THE BUYER ASKS ABOUT YOU, BE HUMBLE, TELL STORIES AND TRY TO BE FUNNY.

"IF I ASK A WOMAN OUT AND SHE HESITATES, I SUGGEST A RESTAURANT I KNOW SHE WILL LIKE. I SWEETEN THE OFFER."

SELLING STRATEGY: IF THE BUYER SAYS HE WILL THINK ABOUT AN OFFER BUT WON'T COMMIT, SWEETEN THE OFFER BY IMPROV-ING THE TERMS. TRY TO GET AN ANSWER BEFORE YOU LEAVE. IT HELPS TO BE VERY SPECIFIC ABOUT YOUR PROPOSAL.

"A MAN WITH BIG MUSCLES IS THINKING WITH HIS ARMS. I LIKE TO THINK WITH MY HEAD. MOST WOMEN PREFER THAT."

SELLING STRATEGY: IT DOESN'T MATTER IF ANOTHER SALES-PERSON HAS MADE A PITCH. IF HE WAS REALLY GOOD, THE DEAL WOULD ALREADY BE DONE. YOU CAN MAKE A DIFFERENCE.

"WOMEN ARE NOT JUST ATTRACTED TO GOOD LOOKS, BUT TO GOOD TIMES. THE SAME IS TRUE FOR ME. IF A WOMAN HAS ONLY LOOKS, I SOON BEGIN TO NOTICE HER IMPERFECTIONS; THERE IS NOTHING ELSE TO KEEP MY ATTENTION."

SELLING STRATEGY: DON'T RELY ON GLITZY POINT-OF-SALE MATERIAL. THAT MAY SPARK AN INITIAL ATTRACTION, BUT YOU HAVE TO GIVE THE BUYER MORE TO COMPLETE THE SALE.

"I ALWAYS ENTER A ROOM BELIEVING IN MYSELF. IF I DON'T BELIEVE IN MYSELF, I CAN'T MAKE A WOMAN BELIEVE IN ME."

SELLING STRATEGY: GO IN POSITIVE. YOU ARE A GREAT SALES-PERSON. LET THE BUYER KNOW HOW EXCELLENT YOU ARE.

"IF A WOMEN IS WITH ANOTHER MAN WHO ARRIVES AFTER I HAVE APPROACHED HER, I APOLOGIZE AND LEAVE. I DON'T IN-TRUDE. I OFTEN COMPLIMENT THE MAN ON HIS DATE AND TELL HIM HOW LUCKY HE IS. I NEVER MAKE A NEGATIVE COMMENT, NO MATTER HOW I FEEL."

SELLING STRATEGY: BE CAREFUL OF CRITICIZING A COMPETI-TOR; IT MAY REFLECT BADLY ON YOU.

"EVERY WOMAN IN A NIGHT SPOT HAS CHOICES. SHE KNOWS IT, AND SO DO YOU. IF THE WOMAN YOU'RE TALKING TO IS LOOK-ING OVER YOUR SHOULDER, CHANGE THE SUBJECT TO GET HER BACK IN THE CONVERSATION."

SELLING STRATEGY: IF YOUR CUSTOMER ISN'T FOCUSING ON

WHAT YOU ARE SAYING, CHANGE GEARS AND TALK ABOUT SOME-
THING THAT GETS HIM TO RESPOND. KEEP HIM CONNECTED.

"I HAVE A 'RAP' FOR VARIOUS TYPES OF WOMEN. THEY HELP ME
CONNECT QUICKLY. ONCE MY RAP IS FINISHED, THEN WE CAN
GET TO KNOW EACH OTHER. A GOOD RAP IS LIKE A KEY TO A
DOOR. DON'T THINK, JUST TAKE THE KEY AND OPEN THE DOOR.
ONCE YOU ARE IN, THEN FIGURE OUT WHAT TO DO."

SELLING STRATEGY: HAVE A NUMBER OF PREPARED STRATE-
GIES. BE STRUCTURED AND CONCISE AND STAY RELEVANT TO THE
BUYER. LET HIM KNOW THAT YOU ARE INFORMED AND ABLE TO
HELP HIM. HOWEVER, PAY ATTENTION TO HIS RESPONSE AND
MAKE SURE YOU GO WITH THE FLOW.

"I HAVE NEVER MET A WOMAN WHO DIDN'T ENJOY A SINCERE
COMPLIMENT."

SELLING STRATEGY: LOOK FOR SOMETHING THAT YOU CAN SIN-
CERELY COMPLIMENT. VALIDATE THE BUYER.

JOAN CASANOVA

"SOME WOMEN ONLY WANT A MAN WHO HAS MONEY. I WANT A
MAN WHO DESERVES MONEY."

SELLING STRATEGY: YOU DON'T NEED A LOT OF SALES EXPERI-
ENCE TO CONVINCE A CUSTOMER THAT YOU HAVE THE COMMIT-
MENT, PREPARATION AND VITALITY TO DO THE BEST JOB.

"I AM LOOKING FOR A MAN WITH PRESENCE. THE ONES I LIKE
BEST ALMOST SEEM TO GLOW."

SELLING STRATEGY: IF YOU WANT TO CONNECT, PUT ON YOUR
MENTAL UNIFORM — BE "WONDERFUL."

"I ALWAYS LOOK AT TEETH, AND WHETHER SHOES ARE SHINED."

SELLING STRATEGY: SHOW YOUR TEETH WITH A SMILE, LOOK INTO THE BUYER'S EYES AND MAKE SURE YOUR SHOES ARE IN GOOD SHAPE. TRUST ME, CUSTOMERS NOTICE.

"IF A MAN FLATTERS ME, I KNOW HE WANTS SOMETHING FROM ME. IF HE COMPLIMENTS ME SINCERELY, I WANT HIM."

SELLING STRATEGY: DON'T USE FLATTERY. LOOK FOR SOMETHING MEANINGFUL TO COMPLIMENT — SOMETHING REAL.

"I AVOID SOMBER MEN LIKE THE PLAGUE. I WANT TO HAVE FUN!"

SELLING STRATEGY: LEAVE YOUR PROBLEMS BEHIND WHEN YOU ARE TALKING TO A CUSTOMER.

"MEN WHO ARE TOO FUNNY GET BORING ALL TOO SOON."

SELLING STRATEGY: EXCESS HUMOR CAN DETRACT FROM PROFESSIONALISM. BE FUNNY, JUST DON'T TAKE IT TO AN EXTREME.

"MEN WHO TALK ONLY ABOUT WORK ARE ALREADY IN A HEAVY RELATIONSHIP. WHY SHOULD I INTERFERE?"

SELLING STRATEGY: TALK ABOUT INTERESTING THINGS, ONLY ONE OF WHICH IS YOUR PROFESSION.

"I'M NOT INTERESTED IN MEN WHO ARE WOMANIZERS. I WANT THE REAL THING."

SELLING STRATEGY: DON'T BE TOO COCKY WHEN YOU PRESENT YOURSELF TO A CUSTOMER. MAKE HIM BELIEVE HE IS IMPORTANT — NOT ONE AMONG MANY.

CHAPTER 12

◢

Reconciling Different Points of View

Reconciling the differences between a buyer and a seller requires that you understand each party's arguments and develop responses to each relevant issue in order to stimulate change.

◢ GATHERING INFORMATION

The first step in reconciling differences between a buyer and a seller is to identify clearly what those differences are.

> Carol, pretend you have an apartment for sale. What price are you asking?
>
> CAROL: *"$1,000,000."*
>
> Diane, you like this apartment and are offering $800,000.
>
> JOHN: *"That offer is too low!"*
>
> Really? What if Carol thinks the apartment's value is $900,000 and is pricing it aggressively to test the market? And what if Diane also sees its value as $900,000 and is offering $800,000 so that she can negotiate to "meet halfway"? That would make $800,000 a very good offer, wouldn't it?
>
> JOHN: *"You're right."*

Good. So what should you do first?

CAROL: *"Submit the offer."*

Of course! But how you submit it is of critical importance, because your initial purpose is not to do the deal but to find out *how* to do the deal.

ROBERT: *"But you have an offer! Don't you have to do your best to get the seller to accept it? Aren't you not doing your job if you don't work the opportunity presented?"*

You don't yet know what opportunity is presented; the seller has to tell you that. You need to fully understand the seller's position consciously and subconsciously.

You can only understand the seller's position by giving him your undivided attention and absorbing his fullest meaning. Remember, your mind can only accept between five and nine bits of information at any one time. If you are thinking about what you are going to say while the seller is talking, you limit the amount of information coming in.

Imagine that you have between five and nine tentacles coming out of your head probing for information. If you are thinking about what you are going to say to the seller — boom! — four tentacles retract. If you start doodling as you talk — boom! — another tentacle is gone. Now you only have between zero and four tentacles left to gather information.

Say the customer speaks, and you hear "No." What good is that? You must know how he said "No." If you don't, you missed all the important stuff! You only listened, you didn't understand!

You deal with this by using a *Script*. That way, you don't have to think about what you are going to say — you just say it. Your tentacles are all out gathering information from the seller; the Script will prompt him to speak.

Be as neutral in your comments as you can. Let the seller stay focused on the offer, not on what he thinks of you and what you said. He should be concentrating on the issues relating to the sale.

Here's a script I often use:

> *Hi, this is [your name] from [name of company]. Do you have a minute?*
>
> *I just received an offer from my buyer in the amount of [amount of offer]. How would you like me to proceed?*
>
> *Well, are you flexible?*
>
> *By how much?*
>
> *Fine, let me call the buyer, and I'll get back to you. Thank you for your time.*

ROBERT: *"What if the seller wants to chat or asks a question?"*
Try as much as possible to stick to the Script. The seller is probably focused on your buyer's offer and is internally processing this information over and over, so much of what you say is peripheral anyway. He is reading his internal book associated with this sale. You want him to keep reading so you can absorb as much of the story as possible and understand his issues and what he will do. You need all your tentacles out to be fully receptive to what he is saying, consciously and subconsciously.

After the next exercise, I want everyone to write down what you think Carol will sell the apartment for. This is not necessarily her stated price, but your best guesses after listening to her with your full attention.

Robert, you be the broker and submit Diane's offer to Carol. Carol, determine what you would be willing to sell for and write it down. This is what you are prepared to accept, not necessarily the price you tell Robert you want.

ROBERT: *"Hi, Carol? This is Robert DiSantis from Bellmarc. Do you have a minute?"*

CAROL: *"Well, maybe just a minute. What is it?"*

Stop. Robert, do you think Carol will be able to give her full attention to what you are about to say?

ROBERT: *"No. She seemed to push me off. I felt rushed."*

What do you think you should do? You need to submit your offer and get as much information from her as you can to understand how to do the deal.

ROBERT: *"Should I suggest that I call at another time?"*

Yes. Say something like: "I'm sorry I'm calling at a bad time. Do you want me to call at a later time?" She will respect your courtesy and be more open to listening to you. Even if she speaks to you immediately, she chose to listen to you.

Okay, let's pretend that Carol has the time to talk now.

ROBERT: *"Hi, Carol? This is Robert DiSantis from Bellmarc. Do you have a minute?"*

CAROL: *"Yes, what is it, Robert?"*

ROBERT: *"I just received an offer on your apartment in the amount of $800,000. How would you like me to proceed?"*

CAROL: *"Don't you think that is too low?"*

ROBERT: *"Well, are you flexible?"*

CAROL: *"I guess I am, but not when the offer is that low."*

ROBERT: *"By how much?"*

CAROL: *"I might be willing to come down by $25,000, but I don't think much more. You know, $800,000 isn't in the ballpark."*

ROBERT: *"Fine, let me call the buyer, and I'll get back to you. Thank you for your time."*

Any questions about the Script?

SYLVIA: *"Don't you think it was a little awkward when he said, 'By how much?'"*

Yes, but consider what is going on for Carol. She is focused on reading her book and going from one page to the other. Robert is reading along with her and asking her questions about its contents. As long as the questions relate to her book, she will continue to focus on it. Carol, were you aware of any awkwardness?

CAROL: *"No, I was just saying things as I was thinking about them."*

Everyone, write down what you think Carol will sell her apartment for.

Robert, now you must call the buyer. Since you have spent some time with her, you should have a sense of how far she would willingly increase her offer. I don't just want you to learn from her response — get her to make that better offer. This figure, the highest the buyer will go without active persuasion, is the "threshold number."

The Script I use is as follows:

Hi, this is [your name] from [name of company]. Do you have a minute?

I submitted your offer to the seller, and he rejected it. However, he said he is flexible and is willing to reduce the price to [the seller's reduced price]. How would you like me to proceed?

Give me [the threshold number].

Fine, let me call the seller, and I'll get back to you. Thank you for your time.

ROBERT: *"If I already have a relationship with the buyer, why do I need to use a script? I already have a sense of her direction."*
Good point. However, things change when you begin negotiations. She may not act the same — be cautious.

DIANE: *"What if the buyer says, 'I don't want to pay any more?'"*
Then you propose the threshold number, unless the customer does it herself or makes an even higher offer.

ROBERT: *"Hi, Diane? This is Robert DiSantis from Bellmarc. Do you have a minute?"*

DIANE: *"Oh, yes, what's going on, Robert?"*

ROBERT: *"I submitted your offer to the seller, and she rejected it. However, she said she is flexible and is willing to reduce the price to $975,000. How would you like me to proceed?"*

DIANE: *"Flexible? That doesn't sound too flexible to me! I guess we have to move on to something else."*

ROBERT: *"Give me $875,000."*

DIANE: *"Why should I come up $75,000 when she came down only $25,000? That doesn't make any sense. No, I don't think so. You tell her that she has to do better than that."*

ROBERT: *"Fine, let me call the seller, and I'll get back to you. Thank you for your time."*

Okay, write down what you think Diane would do the deal for, and tell me what you wrote for both Carol and Diane.

	The Seller: Carol	The Buyer: Diane
John	$925,000	$900,000
Rita	$925,000	$900,000
Sylvia	$910,000	$875,000
Donna	$915,000	$900,000
Robert	$925,000	$900,000

Carol, what did you write down?

CAROL: *"$925,000."*

Diane, what did you write down?

DIANE: *"$900,000. I like the idea of meeting halfway."*

Good, you were all in the ballpark. Let's summarize:

	Expressed Price	Inferred Price
The Seller	$975,000	$925,000
The Buyer	$800,000	$900,000
Difference	$175,000	$25,000

SYLVIA: *"Shouldn't Robert have spent a little time cajoling Diane to raise her offer? He could have gotten her to give him more."*

Yes, but if he did that, what would happen the next time he called?

SYLVIA: *"What do you mean? He would be closer to a deal, wouldn't he?"*

Yes, but he would have created an adversarial environment. The next time he called, Diane would be thinking about how to defend herself before he even started. Because he just sought to gather information and didn't attempt to persuade her, Robert can plan his next call without worrying about resistance. Start the process by letting gravity pull the parties as close as they will come on their own. You want the distance to the edge of the cliff to be as short as possible when you start to push.

IDENTIFY THE UNDERLYING MOTIVATION

The second step in reconciling differences is to identify the underlying motivation in making a decision.

You should call the person with the greater sense of urgency to do the deal; she will be more motivated to increase her offer. If both parties have a similar sense of urgency, decide where you feel value lies. Identify who is closer to your point of view, then call the other person first. Your arguments will be strongest against the person with the weakest position.

Let's say that Robert decides to call the buyer first.

Robert, how are you going to handle that call?

ROBERT: *"Do I identify her hopes and fears?"*

Yes. You already know her short-term objective, her Buying Formula, which is to buy a specific type of apartment at a specific price. Now you need to identify her Middle-Term Objectives, her Purchasing Criteria [*Chapter 8*], which contain the verbs that describe why she wants an apartment in the first place. You identify these verbs by asking, "What are your hopes in buying an apartment?" and "What are your fears in buying an apartment?"

SYLVIA: *"Doesn't it seem a little contrived?"*

Yes, especially since you would have been searching for the buyer's hopes and fears from the beginning. When you first met, you should have asked the buyer, "What do you like and why?" or "What are you afraid of in buying an apartment? What are your concerns?" and if the buyer rejected other apartments, you would have asked why.

When the buyer speaks, focus on the verbs, not just the nouns. Keep probing to develop a list of hopes and fears that you can convert to a Purchasing Criteria list.

Ask the seller similar questions: "How did you choose your asking price? What is the foundation for your position?" Her answers will help you understand her arguments and motivations.

Robert, why don't you call Diane?

ROBERT: *"What are your hopes in buying an apartment?"*

DIANE: *"I want a good deal so I can save money."*

ROBERT: *"So you hope to save. What other hopes do you have?"*

DIANE: *"I really want convenient public transportation."*

ROBERT: *"So you hope for convenience. Any other hopes?"*

DIANE: *"I want a good view."*

ROBERT: *"Why?"*

DIANE: *"Because it makes me tranquil. I feel at peace when I have a good view."*

ROBERT: *"Is it more to feel tranquil or to feel at peace?"*

DIANE: *"To feel tranquil."*

ROBERT: *"Any other hopes?"*

DIANE: *"I hope I can make friends."*

ROBERT: *"Any others?"*

DIANE: *"Not that I can think of."*

ROBERT: *"Do you have any fears in buying an apartment?"*

DIANE: *"I am afraid I'll make a wrong decision and lose money."*

ROBERT: *"Any other fears?"*

DIANE: *"Yes, I want it to be safe."*

ROBERT: *"Any others?"*

DIANE: *"No, I don't think so."*

ROBERT [To the class]: *"I have written up the following hopes and fears"*:

HOPES	FEARS
• To save	• To lose
• To have convenience	• To be safe
• To feel tranquil	
• To make friends	

ROBERT [To the class]: *"When I convert the negative 'fears' into 'hopes,' the criteria list is as follows"*:

PURCHASING CRITERIA LIST
- To save
- To have convenience
- To feel tranquil
- To make friends
- To profit
- To be safe

℘ IDENTIFY MEANINGFUL RESPONSES

The third step in reconciling differences is to identify new information that is relevant to the buyer's Purchasing Criteria.

Now we have Diane's recipe for how she will buy an apartment. These are her underlying motivations. Diane has said that given the facts as she now knows them the apartment is worth only $800,000. This means that:

- Given the amount she believes she can save, this apartment is worth only $800,000.
- Given the level of convenience she is aware of, this apartment is worth only $800,000.
- Given the tranquility she believes the apartment provides, it is worth only $800,000.
- Given where she thinks the opportunity to make friends is, this apartment is worth only $800,000.
- Given the profit she believes she can make, this apartment is worth only $800,000.
- Given her perception of safety in the area, this apartment is worth only $800,000.

As you can see, each item is open to argument. New information on one or more items can change Diane's valuation. These are the issues you need to address to get her to raise her offer. If you give her new information, she will factor it into her decision-making process and draw new conclusions.

You need to try to offer the buyer new information on each criterion. As we discussed earlier [*Chapter 11*], there are three kinds of new information: Substantive, Reframed and Psychological. Try to develop as much pertinent new information as you can so that the buyer can make the most meaningful reassessment.

> Let's start with "to save." What new facts might you explore?
>
> ROBERT: *"This apartment has a low maintenance. Diane will be saving on monthly expenses."*
>
> Is this new information for her?
>
> ROBERT: *"No."*
>
> Then it is already included in her thinking. Anyone else?
>
> SYLVIA: *"This building hasn't had a maintenance increase in five years. It is financially secure and unlikely to make future increases, so she can save."*
>
> Good. The building's ability to maintain itself without maintenance increases is Substantive Information. Now that we have identified a new fact, let's try a Reframe. Any ideas?
>
> DONNA: *"Isn't it great that you're concerned about saving. That means you have looked carefully at your choices and know that this is fairly priced."*
>
> That's a nice Reframe, but it doesn't motivate her to pay more, does it?
>
> DONNA: *"No, not really."*
>
> Okay, can you think of another Reframe?

DONNA: *"Nothing comes to mind."*

Then let's pass on a Reframe for this criterion and think about how we can persuade her using Psychological Information.

JOHN: *"How about Scarcity: 'We have been looking for more than six months, and this is the first apartment that's a serious candidate. Prices are appreciating quickly, and it may take a while to find another. What is your time worth?'"*

Good. We have addressed Diane's wish to save with a new fact and new Psychological Information, but passed on a Reframe.

SYLVIA: *"Wait a second. That psychological information didn't really relate to saving."*

You want to think about Diane's motivations in the broadest possible terms. Saving time is a form of saving. Her time has value to her, even if it isn't strictly monetary.

Let's go to Diane's second criterion, "convenience." What would be a good new fact?

SYLVIA: *"A new gourmet food market is opening down the street."*

Good.

JOHN: *"But Diane wanted convenient transportation. She didn't say anything about food."*

That's true, but as with saving, you need to consider this term as flexibly as possible. Don't limit yourself. If one kind of convenience is meaningful to her, another may be as well. Think about a tree. If you stay near the trunk, there are many branches, but if you go out on a limb you can get stuck. If you define convenience strictly in terms of transportation, you have chosen one limb of the tree. It might be more fruitful to consider all kinds of convenience.

Diane, would a new gourmet food store opening nearby have value to you as an added convenience?

DIANE: *"Absolutely."*

Good, let's go on to a Reframe. If the apartment is convenient enough to be worth $800,000, then how can we make it convenient enough to be worth more?

JOHN: *"I can't think of anything."*

Okay — no Reframe for this criterion either. Is there Psychological Information we can use?

JOHN: *"How about Consistency? Say this apartment has all the features she has asked for. You could say, 'This is the type of apartment you always wanted — now you can get what you asked for.'"*

I'll buy that.

Let's move on to the next criterion, "to feel tranquil."

RITA: *"I can't think of a new fact, but I can think of a Reframe: 'It's great that you yearn to feel tranquil, because in this apartment, with all the energy of New York City around you, you can close your door and experience quiet and peace. You have the best of both worlds.' And for Psychological Information, I would use Social Proof: 'Your friends are going to love visiting you because your apartment will have a sense of peace and tranquility that they will enjoy.'"*

Good. Let's do the next criterion, "to make friends."

ROBERT: *"A new fact might be that the apartment is close to the Metropolitan Museum of Art, which has events where you can meet people and socialize. For a Reframe, I might say: 'Isn't it great that you are moving to a new apartment! There will be a whole set of new people to meet who will be as excited to know you as you are to know them.' I might use Authority as my Psy-*

chological Information and say: 'I know what happens when people move to new homes. Everyone in the building wants to meet them. In my experience as a broker, buyers have been amazed by how many people in their buildings are eager to say hello.'"

Good. Let's do the next criterion, "to profit."

RITA: *"For Substantive Information, I might say that prices increased 5% last year and that demand is pushing prices higher. For a Reframe, I might say: 'Isn't it great, you can invest your money in your home and profit from an improved lifestyle every day. Profit is about living better, not just accumulating money.' For Psychological Information, I might use Scarcity: 'There is a limited supply, so demand will cause prices to increase.'"*

JOHN: *"But we already used Scarcity. Does it make sense to use it again?"*

Of course. Sometimes repetition in different contexts serves to strengthen the argument.

Who wants to handle the last criterion, "safety"?

RITA: *"For a new fact, I would say that all the buildings on the street have doormen."*

Doesn't the buyer know that?

RITA: *"I guess she would, so I have no new facts. But I can do a Reframe: 'It's good that you are concerned about safety, however safety is an issue anywhere in New York City. It's part of the excitement of cosmopolitan living. It's never totally safe but it's never boring.' For Psychological Information I would use Affinity: 'I have lived here for 10 years and raised my children here. I wouldn't live in an unsafe place any more than you would.'"*

Good, now let's list our new points for each criterion:

CRITERION	STATEMENT
To save	NEW FACT No maintenance increase in 5 years. REFRAME — PERSUASION Scarcity: It took six months to find the apartment, and prices are appreciating. Value of your time.
To have convenience	NEW FACT New gourmet food store opening. REFRAME — PERSUASION Consistency: Everything you want is here.
To feel tranquil	NEW FACT — REFRAME You can enjoy the vibrancy of NYC or shut it out by closing your door. PERSUASION Social Proof: Friends will love the feeling of tranquility you will create here.
To make friends	NEW FACT Metropolitan Museum of Art nearby with good social opportunities. REFRAME Your neighbors will be as excited to meet you as you are to meet them. PERSUASION Authority: In my experience as a broker, people always want to meet new owners in their building.
To profit	NEW FACT Prices increased 5% last year; demand pushing prices higher. REFRAME Profit in improved lifestyle every day. PERSUASION Scarcity: Limited supply will cause prices to go up.

To be safe   NEW FACT —

REFRAME Dynamic environment vs. safety.

PERSUASION Affinity: My children grew up in this neighborhood.

❧ PLANNING WHAT TO SAY

You now have new information and arguments for each criterion to get the buyer to reconsider. However, this is the raw data; you need a simplified version, a *Dialogue Guide*, to help you practice your arguments and keep on track during your conversation with your customer. List the criteria, and next to each, write key words that remind you of your new facts and arguments.

Your Dialogue Guide might look like this:

SAVE: Maintenance — 5 years / Scarcity — 6 months / Appreciation, Value of time

CONVENIENCE: Gourmet food store / Consistency — Everything is here

TRANQUIL: It exists — close door / Friends love peace

FRIENDS: Museum / New apartment — Neighbors excited to meet / Authority — People want to meet

PROFIT: Prices up 5%, still pushing / Profit in improved lifestyle every day / Limited supply

SAFE: Dynamic environment vs. safety / Children grew up here

Now you have to practice your arguments so you have control over your material. Try them out on another person and see if they sound right. Notice which words are turn-offs and turn-ons. Develop confidence in what you are going to say.

Robert, why don't you try it with our sample Dialogue
Guide?

ROBERT: *"I want to talk to you about your offer. First, I would
like to tell you how you can save by buying this apartment.
There hasn't been a maintenance increase in this building in five
years. Obviously, the building is careful in spending its money.
Right now there is a tremendous scarcity of apartments like
this. It took you six months to find this one, and it could take six
months to find another, and the market's appreciating. Is it
worth your time and the risk of prices going up to look for something else?*

*"The second point I would like you to consider is conven-
ience. Did you know that a gourmet food store is opening up
down the street? You will now be able to find gourmet prepared
foods practically at your door; you really do have everything you
need right here. It is exactly what you've said you wanted.*

*"I know you want a tranquil atmosphere when you get
home, and that feeling of peace exists here. Just close the door
and the stress of the day will vanish. I'm sure that after you buy
this apartment, your friends will love to come over just because
of the serenity you will create here.*

*"However, if you want to meet new people, this apartment is
close to the Metropolitan Museum of Art. It hosts lots of events,
and it's one of the best places in New York to make friends. I also
know that people in the building will be excited to meet you. In
my experience, when new owners move into a building everyone
wants to get to know them — I see this all the time.*

*"I'm sure you want to make a profit, and all I can say is that
prices rose 5% last year and demand is pushing them even higher. You should also think about another form of profit — the
profit of living better every day. Your lifestyle will surely be better here. Remember, there is a limited supply of these apart-*

*ments because they are desirable. You're lucky — you're here
first; you're the one who has the chance to buy this scarce com-
modity. Such a chance may not come again soon, and limited
supply should keep the price high for when you want to sell.*

*"Finally, I know you are concerned about safety. Well, that's
a reasonable concern. However, safety is an issue everywhere in
New York City; that's just part of living in such a dynamic environment. All I can say is that I have lived in this neighborhood
for 10 years and raised my children here, and I am as concerned
about safety as you are. I wouldn't live here if I thought it were
unsafe."*

Good. Questions?

SYLVIA: *"Does he recite this when he gets on the phone with
Diane?"*

No. The recitation is only preparation. It clarifies what you
want to say. Once you are satisfied with your recitation,
you have to consider what approach to use, how to get
your arguments into a conversation with the buyer and
how to close the call.

❧ CONSIDERING THE APPROACH

You walk into the buyer's Library and see her focused on reading a
book. You want to get her attention. Unless you can get her to switch
her attention from her book to what you have to say, your efforts will be
wasted.

How do you do this? You must approach her tactfully yet decisive-
ly. You must get her attention in a way that either gets her to respond
favorably or confuses her. If she is confused, she will be willing to learn.
Either way, you can connect to a common purpose.

Pretend the sale is a football game and you are the offense. You have the ball and want to score in the buyer's territory. There is a line of resistance, so you must have a plan to succeed. It could be a direct assault through the line, a feint in one direction with a charge in another, a decoy sent into the buyer's territory or a run for limited yardage. Each play is a strategy to overcome a defense.

Direct Approach

In a *Direct Approach*, the salesperson goes right to his argument.

EXAMPLE: Sam Salesperson calls Bob Buyer and says: "I spoke to the seller, and he lowered his price to $125,000. I want to discuss this with you so we can figure out what to do."

Feint

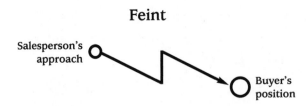

In a *Feint*, the salesperson starts with an irrelevant matter to establish nonconfrontational dialogue. In mid-conversation, he changes to a direct approach.

EXAMPLE: Sam Salesperson calls Bob Buyer and tells him about a restaurant he has gone to. He says, "You know Bob, I really like good Chinese food, and I know you do too." Bob responds with his own favorite restaurants, and they continue on this topic until Sam Salesperson says: "Hey, Bob, I have something else to talk to you about. I spoke to the seller of the apartment you made an offer on, and he has given me some ideas. Would you like me to continue?"

Decoy

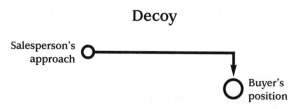

In a *Decoy*, the salesperson brings up a relevant side issue, like the effect of interest rates or buyer demand, and tries to gain negotiating points in this side discussion to attack the buyer's position.

EXAMPLE: Sam Salesperson calls Bob Buyer and says, "Bob, did you see the article in *The New York Times* on Sunday about how the market is tightening?" When Bob says yes, Sam says: "You know, it's becoming harder and harder to find reasonably priced properties. Have you found that to be true too?" When Bob answers yes, Sam says: "Bob, you know that apartment you're considering? I think it might be a good time to make a stronger offer. The seller is still showing flexibility, but it's only a matter of time before he realizes that the market trend is in his favor. You know, Bob, I am having a really hard time finding good properties to show you. You read it in *The New York Times,* and you know it from your own experience. Let's jump at this opportunity."

Limited Engagement

You use a *Limited Engagement* when you believe that the span between the buyer's and seller's positions is too great to cross in one attempt. You are looking for a compromise that will form the basis of a later approach. The parties must be brought together in stages.

EXAMPLE: Sam Salesperson calls Bob Buyer and says: "Bob, you know I think your offer of $300,000 was a good effort, but the seller has advised me that it is too low for him to make a counteroffer. I propose that you raise your bid to $350,000. I believe the seller will then make a constructive counteroffer for us to evaluate."

✎ SELECTING THE RIGHT APPROACH

Before choosing your approach, analyze what you know about the buyer. Step out of yourself and imagine her responses to the different techniques. Picking the wrong approach can be dangerous; picking the right one can move you closer to achieving your goal.

> SYLVIA: *"What if you don't know which approach to take?"*
> Then I generally use a Direct Approach. However, normally it is not difficult to step into your buyer's shoes and figure out which strategy will suit her best.

✎ CREATING CONVERSATION

If you present your argument and the buyer doesn't respond, you don't know how much information she absorbed. Try marking your Dialogue Guide with points where you will look for a response. Put in questions like: "Do you agree?" "What do you think?" "Does what I say make sense?" or "Does this matter to you?"

> ROBERT: *"What if the customer gives you yes or no answers and you know there is more there than she is saying?"*
> Try *Backtracking* [*Chapter 4*]: repeat her last sentence and affirm her concerns. This will help pace the conversation and will feel good to the buyer. You can also say: "Gee, I see you have some reservations. Why don't you give me a fuller sense of your concerns?" Bring the buyer in as much as you

can. Make sure she is processing whatever you are saying and not just receiving it. You want more than just a superficial response.

I recommend treating each criterion as a module: start by stating the criterion word, then your position, then elicit a response from the buyer. If the response is superficial, you should keep probing. You are trying to get the customer to process the information fully and give you meaningful responses.

℅ THE CLOSING REMARK

Be clear about what your goal is before initiating the conversation. Your first goal should be to get the seller's expressed price. If that can't be achieved, attempt to get the seller's inferred price, and if that is not viable, attempt to get the buyer's inferred price. Your backup plan should be to get a new offer that keeps the momentum of negotiations going. Always try to get something.

℅ FINALIZING YOUR PLAN

Now you can create a full negotiating plan. Robert, show us what your plan looks like.

Plan for Negotiating with Diane, the Buyer

	Expressed Price	Inferred Price
The Seller	$975,000	$925,000
The Buyer	$800,000	$900,000
Difference to Reconcile	$175,000	$25,000

INTRO: Direct Approach

SAVE: Maintenance — 5 years / Scarcity — 6 months, Appreciation, Value of time — I'm sure you see value in this

CONVENIENT: Gourmet food store / Everything is here — Don't you agree?

TRANQUIL: It exists — close door / Friends will love peace

FRIENDS: Museum to meet / New apartment — neighbors excited to meet/ Authority — People want to meet — You know you will meet people, don't you?

PROFIT: Prices up 5%, still pushing / Profit in improved lifestyle every day / Limited supply — Don't you agree?

SAFE: Dynamic environment vs. safety / Children grew up here

CONCLUSION: Let's really make an effort to make this happen. Make an offer the seller can accept so we can take advantage of this.

TARGET: $975,000; then $925,000; then $900,000.

Now what do you do with this Negotiating Plan?

ROBERT: *"Call Diane and go through it with her."*

And what if you start talking about saving, your first criterion, and she veers off the topic?

ROBERT: *"I guess I have to respond to what she wants to talk about. I can't go through my arguments in the order I wrote them."*

That's important. You are not reciting what you have written; you are using it as a basis for exploring the buyer's issues and presenting information. If she wants to talk about things that are not on your plan or are out of order, be flexible and focus on her concerns.

Is there anything else?

ROBERT: *"Like what?"*

You may be missing something you can't even verbalize. Check in with your subconscious; the plan must feel right.

ROBERT: *"It does."*

How does it feel to Diane? You'd better find out before you call her. Project how this call will make her feel and what she will do.

ROBERT [After thinking about it]: *"Well, I think she will agree to $900,000, but I know she is going to worry about going higher."*

How should you handle that?

ROBERT: *"I shouldn't push her too hard until I am clear that only a small amount more would make the deal succeed."*

Okay. Now step back and look from the triangular position. See you and Diane having this conversation. Do you notice anything?

ROBERT: *"I think she is going to fight me."*

How should you deal with that?

ROBERT: *"I guess I should agree with her a lot, so she feels affirmed and understood. I should also Backtrack and repeat back to her what she says to me. I think she'll like that."*

Good. Now think in terms of the big picture. Step above the two of you [*Chapter 6*].

ROBERT [After thinking about it]: *"I think I'd better remember that if this doesn't work out I don't have anything else to show her. I'd better make sure she remembers that too."*

Good. This is the most important part of negotiating a deal — stepping back at the end and taking stock of what is going on for you and for the customer. You must believe the scenario will work. If it doesn't feel right, don't make the call — think some more. You don't have to be certain of the outcome, just that your plan is the best alternative available.

You have considered the Reader and the Observer. Does the Higher Self at the door of the Library have anything to say about this?

ROBERT [Pausing for reflection]: *"No."*

Okay, Robert, time to call.

ROBERT: *"Hi, Diane? Do you have a minute?"*

DIANE: *"Sure, Robert. What is it? Did you talk to the seller about that apartment?"*

ROBERT: *"You know, I haven't spoken to her, but I'm sure she will come down, and I thought if we discussed it a bit more we might be able to come up with a good strategy."*

DIANE: *"I don't know. It doesn't look like there is going to be a deal here."*

ROBERT: *"You're right, there are some problems. However, there are some important things you should consider. I know you are concerned about saving. This building hasn't had a maintenance increase in five years. To me, that means the building is in good financial condition and has control over its costs. I also know you have been looking for more than six months. That's a long time. What you want is very scarce. Besides, what is the value of your time? I'm sure you see the value in pursuing this."*

DIANE: *"All right, what do you want me to do?"*

ROBERT: *"Ideally, I would like you to say: 'Okay, I'll increase my bid. Let's get this show on the road!'"*

DIANE: *"At $975,000? You must be kidding."*

ROBERT: *"I understand you think I'm kidding, and yet there is some basis for increasing your offer. You want to get a good value and to make a profit if you eventually sell. Prices have risen 5% this year and are still going up. And you should consider the profit of having a better lifestyle. Profit is more than just economics; it's also how you're living your life. There is a limited supply, and you have an opportunity. Don't you agree?"*

DIANE: *"I will only agree to what I can afford. I'm not sure I can afford this."*

ROBERT: *"I respect your concern about affordability, though I'm sure you know that everyone stretches to move into a new* *home. Look, this place is very convenient. They're opening a new gourmet food store nearby. Everything is here, don't you agree? What about an offer that's a compromise? Would you give me, say, $925,000?"*

DIANE: *"Great, a new food store. But what about what's fair? She's not in the ballpark!"*

ROBERT: *"She's not in the ballpark right now, but we can bring her there if we play our cards right. This place is special, Diane. Don't you see that this is something your friends would love?"*

DIANE: *"Yes, I agree. But I can't justify the money."*

ROBERT: *"Yes, it is a lot of money, and it's worth a lot of money. Diane, as much as your friends would love it, this is also an opportunity to make new friends. You are close to the Metropolitan Museum of Art, which has great activities you can participate in to meet new people. You can also meet new people in the building. In my experience as a broker, your new neighbors will be excited to get to know you. I think you can make an offer that can make it happen."*

DIANE: *"It's just too high for me."*

ROBERT: *"Okay, how about $900,000?"*

DIANE: *"That's more than I want to pay."*

ROBERT: *"Diane, prices have risen 5% this year so far. If you don't buy this, the next one might be more expensive. I know this area. I raised my children here. It's wonderful and safe. You will be happy here."*

DIANE: *"Okay, offer her $900,000, and that's it."*

ROBERT: *"Let me see what I can do."*

What did you think of Robert's performance?

SYLVIA: *"I was very surprised that he suggested offers in the middle of the conversation. I thought he would make suggestions at the end."*

Remember, the plan is just an outline.

Say I begin a painting with a specific form in mind; I even draw it on the canvas before I apply paint. That outline is just the beginning; it is not the final picture. Your conversation with the buyer is like doing the painting; you must use all your talents to paint a creative, exciting picture. While it is important to have the picture as clear as possible in your mind before you begin, the finished product will be different than you imagined it.

Once your conversation with the customer has begun, let it develop on its own. Negotiate from your subconscious. You have prepared for the dance, and you know all the steps, now move with the rhythm of the music. Be in the State of Selling [*Chapter 2*].

CAROL: *"But Robert added things that weren't on the outline and didn't hit all the points he intended to cover."*

That's okay. He used his full awareness and explored subjects as they came up. Suppose that in the middle Diane had said, "Gee, that's great, let's do the deal!" would you have continued presenting all the points on the outline?

CAROL: *"Of course not. I would have met my goal."*

Exactly. The objective is clear, but the process is variable. Don't be hung up on your outline. It helps you get ready, but it shouldn't limit you.

Also, don't rush your words. If you do, you won't have time to think as you speak. Take time to feel the conversation and become aware of its rhythm and language. Every piece of music has a pace; if it is played too quickly it loses its appeal. Consider speaking contemplatively rather than emphatically.

DIANE: *"I loved when Robert talked about 'playing our cards right' after I said 'out of the ballpark.' He drew me right in. It was just like the Robber Baron model [Chapter 7]."*

All the pieces work together. If you master these techniques, you will have them ready when you need them. Your subconscious will bring them forward as needed if you permit your creative part to express itself.

RITA: *"Are there any shortcuts to this process?"*

It is useful to develop models for imaginary "typical customers." Pretend to have a buyer and go through the process. You won't be exactly on target because each person is unique, but you can gather information to address common issues and practice presenting that information. If you are familiar with the process, you will be able to apply it more easily.

❧ SUMMARY

This is the chapter in which everything comes together and you learn how to apply your knowledge in a negotiation. You are given a sample script for submitting an offer to a seller; a sample script for eliciting the buyer's response; a way to use either party's hopes and fears to develop *Purchasing Criteria*; a strategy for developing effective and convincing arguments; and suggestions for how to present your arguments so that they will be understood and processed.

SYLVIA: *"What is the script for submitting an offer to a seller?"*

Hi, this is [your name] from [your company]. Do you have a minute?

I just received an offer from my buyer in the amount of [amount of offer]. How would you like me to proceed?

Well, are you flexible?

By how much?

Fine, let me call the buyer, and I'll get back to you. Thank you for your time.

ROBERT: *"What is the script for getting the buyer's retort to the seller's response?"*

Hi, this is [your name] from [your company]. Do you have a minute?

I submitted your offer to the seller, and he rejected it. However, he said he is flexible and is willing to reduce the price to [seller's price]. How would you like me to proceed?

Give me [threshold number].

Fine, let me call the seller, and I'll get back to you. Thank you for your time.

CAROL: *"What is your objective when you submit an offer?"*

To learn from the seller's response what his position is and how to make a deal.

DIANE: *"What is the threshold number?"*

It is the highest amount you believe the buyer will offer with no act of persuasion on your part other than a request for that amount.

RENE: *"What are the critical things to do when preparing to persuade?"*

- Identify your buyer's hopes and fears in making the purchase and convert these into a single list of positive verbs (the Purchasing Criteria).
- Provide information in the form of Substantive Information, Reframed information or Psychological Information to address each item on the criteria list.
- Prepare a Dialogue Guide to help you organize your points in the most effective way.
- Practice your presentation.
- Select the approach best suited to your specific buyer.
- Consider how likely the customer will be to respond to

your chosen approach and your arguments and step back and look at the big picture.

- Talk to your customer. Remember, it is a conversation, not a recitation.

- Seek the seller's expressed price, then the seller's inferred price, then the buyer's inferred price. If none of these can be achieved, then get anything you can to maintain momentum.

MICHAEL: *"What is a Dialogue Guide?"*

A Dialogue Guide is a brief outline of your facts and arguments expressed in key words. You use it to practice your presentation and to keep you on track during your conversation with the customer.

SYLVIA: *"Why should you interpret your buyer's Purchasing Criteria in the broadest possible way?"*

Since you are choosing which arguments to make, you want to interpret the criteria broadly so you have the greatest number of choices in identifying the most persuasive position.

SUSAN: *"What approaches can you use to communicate your argument? When would you use each?"*

DIRECT APPROACH: When the buyer or seller likes direct information and will be open to hearing your argument.

FEINT: When directly communicating your points will turn the listener off, establish a friendly conversation before broaching difficult subjects.

DECOY: Using a relevant side issue to gain negotiating points before tackling the main issue head-on. This should be used when you see an opportunity to diffuse resistance prior to actually discussing the transaction.

LIMITED ENGAGEMENT: When the spread between the buyer's position and seller's position is too great to span in one attempt, take an interim step as part of a total strategy.

CASSANDRA: *"Why is it important to get the buyer or seller to respond to your negotiating points?"*

The listener should process the information you provide, not just listen to it. Getting him to respond will help him connect and keep him engaged while you are speaking.

Go with the Flow

A SALESPERSON IS LIKE THE CAPTAIN OF A SAILING SHIP. THE FASTEST ROUTE TO YOUR GOAL MAY NOT BE A STRAIGHT LINE, AND EVEN THOUGH YOU CHART YOUR COURSE CAREFULLY, CHANGES IN WIND DIRECTION AND VELOCITY MAY COMPEL YOU TO ADJUST YOUR PLANS. AS YOU CHANGE DIRECTION, YOU MUST DO SO CAREFULLY. TO BE RECKLESS COULD CAUSE THE WIND TO CATCH IN YOUR SAILS AND CAPSIZE THE SHIP.

AS YOU HEAD TOWARD YOUR GOAL, YOU MUST KEEP YOUR HAND ON THE WHEEL. NEW WINDS MAY COME OUT OF NO-WHERE TO ALTER YOUR PATH AND DISRUPT YOUR VOYAGE. SOMETIMES, THE WIND SUBSIDES ALTOGETHER, AND YOU MUST WAIT FOR A BETTER TIME TO PICK UP SPEED — YOU MUST REMAIN VIGILANT AND CANNOT GIVE UP. WHEN ON THE OCEAN, YOU HAVE NO CHOICE BUT TO GO ON. THE WIND WILL EVENTUALLY RETURN, AND THE FLEXIBLE CAPTAIN WILL TAKE ADVANTAGE OF IT TO SET A NEW COURSE. YOU NEVER KNOW WHERE THE WIND WILL LEAD YOU, BUT IT WILL ALWAYS COME.

CHAPTER 13

♂

Additional Negotiating Strategies

In Chapter 11, I discussed Persuasive Techniques using the acronym A CARESS (Authority, Consistency, Affinity, Reciprocity, Exclusivity, Scarcity and Social Proof). Here, I give refinements and examples of these core techniques as well as introduce some new ones.

⚜ AUTHORITY

When making an important purchase, you want to make the right decision. But what is right? You search for assurance, endorsement and validation, often asking the advice of an Authority, a person more knowledgeable than yourself whose expertise provides confirmation.

EXAMPLES:

• A seller was unsure about the value of his apartment. A real estate broker trying to get an exclusive listing gave him a business card saying that he was a GRM and a vice president of his company. The seller did not know that GRM was a company designation that required minimal experience and that every salesperson in the company was a vice president. The seller believed that these credentials were meaningful and accepted the broker's pricing recommendations because he saw him as an Authority.

• During negotiations over an apartment, a broker said to the seller: "Look, I've been in business for 15 years. I was here when your building was converted to a cooperative, and I have seen every transaction in the building since. You are getting a good price. Trust me, you should take this offer." The seller accepted the offer.

The moral of the story: Authority is oil to the decision-making machine — it smooths out differences and eases insecurity by giving validation for change.

✺ CONSISTENCY

When confronted with an irregularity in his logic, a customer will usually change his position to restore Consistency.

EXAMPLE:

• A seller verbally accepted a bid on his apartment. However, within a week, he received a higher offer. When he told the broker, the broker said: "You know, I have always felt that you were an honorable person who put a high regard on doing the right thing. In all our dealings, I never asked you to sign a piece of paper. I always believed that your word was your bond. What is the buyer going to think after she trusted me? After I told her that a deal was done and she incurred legal costs as a result? Is it the honorable thing to leave her in the lurch?" The seller stuck with the original deal.

The moral of the story: Consistency is a strong motivator. If your argument is based on getting the customer to remain true to his values and beliefs, you can generally make the deal.

℅ℐℴ **AFFINITY**

Building a relationship with the customer is essential to success. If you create a bond of mutual respect and understanding, the customer will look to you as a trusted confidant, not just as a peddler of wares.

EXAMPLES:

• When a buyer asked his broker what she thought about a proposed bid on an apartment, the broker said: "Before we move on, I want to remind you that I have a vested interest in getting you to buy this apartment. I am getting a commission from the seller. I am reminding you of this because I really want to do the right thing. That said, I think it is an excellent deal at $250,000, and you should feel comfortable with that bid." By giving a disclaimer before her advice, the broker was exploiting her Affinity with the customer. Of course he knew the broker was getting a commission, but the reminder confirmed his sense of her honesty and helped him trust her advice.

• A buyer was very clear that he wanted to live only on the East Side of Manhattan between 73rd and 79th Streets close to Central Park. He had a good relationship with his broker, often mentioning that he enjoyed working with him and trusted him. When the broker wanted him to see an apartment on 63rd Street and Third Avenue, the buyer would not consider it until the broker reminded him of the trust and confidence the buyer had often expressed in his judgment. The buyer looked at the apartment.

The moral of the story: By creating a connection with a customer, you can create commonality of goals.

✎ RECIPROCITY

The Golden Rule, *Do unto others as you would have them do unto you*, has been greatly tested in negotiations. Underlying this rule is its reverse: *Whatever I do for you, I expect the same back*. Working the quid pro quo is an important element in inducing change. An act of compromise demands a similar response from the other party.

EXAMPLES:

• Both parties to an apartment deal were inflexible on the last $10,000. The broker proposed splitting the difference, but both refused. The broker then said to the buyer: "If you come up with a third of the money, I will come up with a third from my commission. For you, it's only about a 3% increase, for me it's a third of my income. I am giving up a third of my income in exchange for 3% from you. How can you say no to that?" The buyer agreed. The broker then told the seller what the buyer had agreed to do and suggested it was only fair that he do the same. The seller agreed.

• An apartment deal hit a snag when the seller wanted to put off the closing for 180 days or until he found another home. The buyer was willing to wait only 60 days. The broker got the seller to agree to a closing in 60 days as long as he could stay longer if necessary. In that event, he would pay rent covering the monthly maintenance charge and the buyer's monthly mortgage payment. The broker then said to the seller, "If you want the buyer to give you both time to stay and below-market rent, what are you going to give the buyer in return?" The seller agreed to a price concession to reciprocate.

The moral of the story: Every action creates an impulse to respond in kind. Reciprocity can be a powerful tool for reconciliation.

⟡ EXCLUSIVITY

Exclusivity is the reason some people buy a Mercedes instead of a Chevrolet. It implies both swank image and better quality. If you can portray a product as exclusive, it becomes desirable. A well-known discotheque was more concerned about having a crowd outside than customers inside. A friend of mine who worked there told me that the single biggest draw for customers was that "you couldn't get in."

EXAMPLES:

• A salesperson had an appointment with an apartment buyer who parked her BMW on the street. The apartment was in an average-looking building, and the first thing the buyer did was measure the living room. She said the apartment was too small. They saw several apartments in the immediate area, but each was "too small." In addition, the salesperson noticed something curious. After each apartment was shown, the customer checked her car to make sure everything was okay. The buyer was a teacher in Brooklyn, and her car was her most prized possession. The salesperson then proposed that they see an apartment that was not on the showing list, but that she thought the buyer might consider.

The customer asked: "Is it big? You know I want the most space possible." The salesperson said: "No, but it is in the Saratoga. Not just any building — the Saratoga!"

The apartment was on a low floor with no view and had significantly less space than others they had seen. The salesperson said: "Is there any reason you shouldn't live in a high-prestige building? The Saratoga is a top-quality building, and you can live in it!" The customer bought the apartment. For her, the Saratoga represented a major step up to a new level of exclusivity.

• My partner and I once wanted to sell an apartment for $125,000, but buyer response was poor. A salesperson proposed that we raise our price. He said that people reading the ad thought that something must be wrong with it at that price, so they didn't call. We raised the price to $200,000 and sold it for $175,000. By raising the price, we made the apartment seem special and unique, increasing demand.

The moral of the story: If you can create an aura of exclusivity, the customer becomes eager to "join the club."

℀ SCARCITY

Scarcity always exists. In a "buyer's market," there is abundant supply but few buyers, so Scarcity motivates sellers to accommodate buyers' demands. In a "seller's market," lots of buyers are chasing a limited supply, putting pressure on buyers to increase their offers and decide quickly. Scarcity increases one party's inflexibility while compelling the other to bend.

EXAMPLES:
• A buyer offered $800,000 for a two-family house. The seller accepted the offer, but the buyer withdrew it after acceptance. The salesperson then persuaded the buyer to offer $750,000, which the seller also accepted, but the buyer again withdrew his bid after it was accepted. At his wit's end, the salesperson asked his company manager to talk to the buyer. The manager called the buyer and said: "You know, I'm really glad you didn't buy that property. It's really important to me to maintain a relationship with you, and let's face it, it is a lot of money. I know a better property will come up eventually, and we can still do business. Besides, now that you have negotiated the price down so low, we have a line of people eager to buy the property. It seems that everybody is happy!" The buyer bought the property for $750,000.

• A salesperson had a buyer looking for a large studio apartment. Every place he saw was too small. Finally, the salesperson showed him a sub-grade basement with a view of a wall, but it was large. The buyer bid $200,000, but the seller said no; he wanted at least $300,000. The salesperson reminded him that this was the first offer in almost a year and that if he did not take it there would be no others. After reflecting on the scarcity of buyers, the seller agreed.

The moral of the story: Scarcity dictates the outcome.

℘ SOCIAL PROOF

We are all social creatures and, to varying degrees, want others to validate our actions. Social Proof is validation by friends, family or anyone whose viewpoint the customer cares about. These people can strongly influence decision-making.

EXAMPLE:

• An insurance broker who wanted to do business with our property-management company met my partner, Marc, and me at our office. He was extremely friendly and said: "Boy, you guys are really growing. I have a friend who now owns a stock brokerage company in New York who started out like you. We fly together to our homes in Aspen, Colorado, during the winter. I should have you meet him. I'm sure you guys would be able to do some deals together."

We talked about our business affairs, and he asked about our property purchases. He said, "You know, my close friend owns the Hyatt Hotel chain and is always looking for real estate deals." Later he said: "I should take you guys to see the chairman of Greater New York Insurance Company. It would be good for you to develop a relationship with him. He is quite a guy. Would you like me to arrange it?" When he left, we were very impressed. Marc said: "This guy is someone to know! I really hope we can give him business." I agreed.

The moral of the story: Other people are a "stamp of approval."

❧ QUICKSAND

One of the oldest games in car sales is bait and switch. The dealer gets the customer into the store by advertising something too good to be true. They negotiate a deal on the promoted vehicle, and the salesperson tells the customer to wait while he arranges for the car to be cleaned and readied for pickup.

The salesperson soon returns with the bad news: The last car they had on sale just sold. However, he says, "for $500 more I can give you another car with more options that's ready to go!"

The customer is upset. He drove all the way over there to make this deal, and now this! Unfortunately, all too often buyers sign the paperwork and fork over the extra money. Why? Quicksand. They got sucked in, and the power of the deal was so strong they couldn't get out. Quicksand is a very powerful strategy.

EXAMPLE:

• My partner, Marc, and I were looking for new office space and thought we found a fantastic deal. The rent was cheap, and the landlord agreed to give us the first seven months rent-free as well as contribute part of the cost of renovations. We were delighted and notified our old landlord that we were leaving.

However, when the new landlord sent the lease to our attorney there were some problems. We were getting four months free, not seven; we had to use the landlord's contractors (who we knew would be more expensive than ours); and any costs over a specified amount would be our responsibility, including the cost of improvements necessary to conform the space to city building codes, costs usually paid by the landlord.

As soon as one item was resolved another would appear. The landlord was not going to provide the cleaning service he had said he would. Our electric bill was going to include a landlord's "add on" on top of the normal rate. Additionally, we would be partly responsible for general improvements to the building. If the building needed a new roof, for example, we would have to pay part of that cost.

We became more and more frustrated — we couldn't get this deal completed. Finally, we heard that the landlord had a partner who was rejecting the settlements we thought we had won. I said to Marc, "Let's dump this deal." He replied: "Neil, we have invested more than $10,000 in legal fees, and our existing lease is about to expire. For us to look for another space now would be crazy." We signed the lease with most of the unfavorable provisions included because we realized we really had no choice — we were in quicksand.

The moral of the story: Once you step into quicksand it's hard to get out.

✈ DIPLOMACY

Did you ever wonder what diplomats do when they enter into negotiations? Conversations last for days, weeks, even years. Is there that much to talk about? Yes, because the process is as much a part of the objective as the final conclusion is. The goal is to develop agreement about more and more things.

When a disagreement arises, the diplomats put the subject aside and move on to another matter on which the parties can agree. As the process moves forward, points of flexibility are discovered and areas of intransigence are identified and carefully explored. As areas of agreement accumulate, ideas germinate that may form the basis for later compromise.

EXAMPLES:

• A salesperson working on an apartment deal hit a snag: The buyer insisted that the deal include the apartment's built-ins, and the seller refused. The buyer also insisted that the seller replace the stove, which he claimed was not working properly. The salesperson asked the buyer, "Assuming you get what you want, what are you willing to pay?" The buyer answered, "$350,000." The salesperson then asked the seller, "If the buyer was willing to pay you $20,000 for the built-ins, would that be fair?" The seller said yes. The salesperson then asked, "If the buyer bid $330,000 for the apartment and $20,000 for the built-ins for a total of $350,000, would you accept?" The seller said yes. No mention was ever again made of the stove.

• A salesperson working on a deal once told me there were dozens of issues in the way. I asked him what the offer was. He said there was no offer yet; the deal was in the "preliminary" stage. I asked, "What does the seller want?" He said, "$300,000." I asked, "Would the buyer pay that if all the issues were out of the way?" He didn't know. I suggested that he find out what the buyer would pay if all the issues were resolved in his favor. He could then adjust the price to reflect the value of the side issues. The salesperson took my suggestion, and the transaction was quickly completed with only minor price adjustments.

The moral of the story: Diplomacy is the art of getting people to say "yes." Don't spin your wheels working on the "nos." Build on the points of consensus; they will illuminate the path to resolving the more difficult issues.

⁓ AND YET...

We all want to explain the logic behind our points of view. We are sure that if we do, our good sense will be clear and any reasonable person will change his position to fit ours. However, the other person's reasoning may be totally different. Sometimes it pays to just remain silent or pose the appropriate question and let the other person come to the logical conclusion on his own.

EXAMPLES:

• I once wanted to buy a property from a man who was in financial difficulty and at risk of losing everything. He gave me his list of demands, some of which were utterly absurd. I stared at him and slowly said, "Tell me, what will happen if we do not do this deal?"

• A famous New York real estate developer once told me a story about the first time he bought a building from Harry Helmsley. In his day, Harry Helmsley was the best there was. The young man was led into Harry's office while Harry was on the phone. Harry continued to talk as the young man listened. When Harry was done with the call he asked, "What is it you want?" The young man said he wanted to buy a building that Harry was offering for $1,000,000.

When the young man was done, Harry said nothing. He just stared at him. The young man grew uncomfortable, and said after a period of silence, he would be willing to spend $800,000 to buy the building. Harry said nothing, just looked down at his yellow pad and began to write. Not a word. The young man said he would pay $900,000. Harry looked up; then his head went back down as he continued to write. Finally, the young man said he would pay $950,000. Harry looked up, pressed his intercom button and told his secretary to tell his attorney to write the contract.

I heard this story many years later when that young man had become a famous real estate developer in his own right. He said that Harry was the toughest negotiator he had ever met because he never told you what he would do. He always let you figure it out for yourself, and you would always overpay.

The moral of the story: Silence can be golden.

❧ FAIT ACCOMPLI

When something unclear is presented as fact, the negotiator is trying to make it a *fait accompli*. If the other person buys into his "fact," there will be one less thing to negotiate.

EXAMPLE:

• A recently engaged couple was looking for an apartment to be their home. The woman liked a number of choices, but her fiancée found reasons, sometimes bordering on the ridiculous, to kill each deal. He was obviously having cold feet about more than buying an apartment.

I said to the man: "The price of apartments is crazy, isn't it? You guys are trying to buy a one-bedroom apartment, and you have to spend $350,000. Isn't it ridiculous?" He agreed, and said he wasn't sure it was worth it. I said: "Let's look at some facts. For one, you are both young, and your income-producing years are ahead of you. You will earn at least 10% more next year than this year and significantly more in the years beyond. That's a fact!" He agreed. I said: "It's also a fact that you are not a kid anymore, and you have to accept that reality. You are at that next stage, when change is upon you. It's a fact. It's time to change." He nodded. Then I added: "It's also a fact that whatever you buy will not make you happy. To be happy, you need five times more space than you can afford." He again agreed. Then I said: "Okay, let's

239

look at where you are. You must change. However, whatever decision you make won't be for forever — it is only the beginning. The important thing right now is to make your fiancée happy. That, too, is a fact." He paused and thought about what I said. They bought the next apartment she liked.

The moral of the story: Creating facts makes for less uncertainty. Define side issues as "givens" so everyone can focus on the main points.

✎ GOOD GUY/BAD GUY

One of the most commonly used sales techniques is "Good Guy/Bad Guy." One partner plays an uncooperative pessimist and the other a hopeful, cooperative optimist. The optimist appears to want to accommodate the buyer but is constrained by the uncooperative pessimist. The bad guy can be your manager, your spouse, your partner or any other participating third party. It can even be your company and its policies. Playing the good guy and using someone else to get your point across can be powerful without being offensive.

EXAMPLES:

• Years before we met, my partner, Marc, wanted to buy a building in Florida. The seller wanted $2.5 million, and Marc negotiated hard to get the price down to $2.3 million. He went to his father, who was funding the deal, but his father refused to pay Marc's negotiated price. He told Marc to offer $1.5 million. Marc did, and the seller was furious.

Marc told him he was sorry. He said he had thought everything was fine, but his father valued the property differently. Marc said he would do whatever he could because he felt terrible about disappointing the seller after they had agreed on a price. With Marc as the good guy and his father as the bad guy, they settled the deal for $2.1 million.

240

The moral of the story: Acting as a good guy being constrained by a bad guy allows you to demand concessions and still be sympathetic. You can have significant disagreement without personal anger.

❦ PRICE VS. TERMS

Often a buyer or seller becomes fixated on a price and is completely inflexible. It may be best to agree to the price and look for concessions on the terms, which can include the time and method of payment.

EXAMPLES:

• A seller wanted $150,000 and wouldn't take less. The buyer agreed to $150,000 on the condition that he get a bank mortgage for $100,000 and pay the additional $50,000 to the seller over 10 years in equal install-ments with no interest. The seller agreed, since he got $150,000.

• A seller had a mortgage of $250,000 and wouldn't sell for less. The buyer wouldn't pay more than $225,000. The deal was struck with the buyer renting the apartment for $1 for a year and then, at the end of the year, buying it for $250,000. Since the unit had a monthly rental value of $2,000, the buyer got $24,000 in value by living in it essentially rent-free for a year. The seller got his price; the buyer got her terms.

The moral of the story: When a seller insists on too high a price, maybe you can make it work by getting concessions on the terms.

❦ PERSUASIVE WORDS

Certain words and phrases are persuasive, others are not. Persuasive words create a conciliatory environment and encourage flexibility.

They include "fair," "equal," "just," "good," "it's what's right," "I understand" and "at your service."

EXAMPLE:

• A salesperson said to her buyer: "Sir, all the seller is looking for here is a fair deal. He wants a deal that is equitable and just for everybody. I know you understand and that you can sympathize with his desire to do what's right. He is seeking your help. He will be fair to you, and you should be fair to him."

The moral of the story: You catch more flies with honey than with vinegar. Sprinkle some persuasive words into your argument to make the taste more appealing to your buyer.

✲ CREATE AN AUCTION

I have always been amazed at the enthusiasm of bidders at auctions. Auctions create energy. When a sale becomes a competition, no one wants to lose. An auction can give you a significant edge.

EXAMPLE:

• A buyer made an offer of $320,000 on an apartment with an asking price of $375,000. When the salesperson told him that another buyer had just bid $350,000, he raised his offer to $355,000. When the broker said the other party had increased his bid to $365,000, the buyer answered with $375,000. When the other bidder went up to $380,000, the buyer bid $385,000. Sold! The broker called to congratulate the buyer on his purchase of the apartment at $385,000.

The moral of story: When you create an auction, the beast has a mind of its own, but wherever it goes will be to the seller's advantage.

❧ CLARITY

One of the most difficult aspects of brokering a transaction is identifying the primary issues within the quagmire of things said by the buyer and seller. Focusing on the fundamentals will usually resolve peripheral issues. Clarity can be found in a number of ways:

CONCEPT 1: *The Money* — Price is fundamental to most negotiations. Ask yourself if the other issues can be resolved with a price adjustment. Usually, after the dust settles, it's all about money.

CONCEPT 2: *See the Big Picture* — Deals often get derailed by minor details. Step back and look at the overall objective, not just the specifics.

CONCEPT 3: *Understand the Whys* — Don't just look at the parties' actions, try to understand the reasons behind them. Why is someone taking a specific position? What is the meaning behind the statements?

If you can create clarity by defining the goal and issues, you can direct the negotiation in a productive way.

EXAMPLES:

• A buyer was considering two apartments with similar layouts in the same brownstone. One was on the fourth floor, the other was on the second. She first saw the second-floor apartment, which was selling for $350,000. She liked it but could not afford it. The broker then asked what she would be willing to give up if he could get her the same apartment for $250,000. "Would you give up some light, location, maybe some room?" The buyer said no. The salesperson then said, "Would you give more effort?" He took her to the fourth-floor apartment and said: "This apartment is $100,000 less, but it requires more effort. Is it worth it for $100,000?" After going up and down the stairs six times, she decided it was and made the offer.

• A buyer wanted an apartment with a terrace. His salesperson showed him two similar apartments, one with a terrace and one without, and said: "You should know what the apartment costs and what the terrace costs. The apartment without the terrace is $150,000, the one with the terrace is $200,000. Therefore, a terrace will cost you $50,000. Do you want a $150,000 apartment with a $50,000 terrace, or would you prefer a better apartment with no terrace for $200,000?"

The moral of the story: Clarity provides a shining light that often reveals the path to success for a deal.

🎵 TIME

If you try to build momentum, the customer may feel pressured. If you give the customer time to think, opportunities slip away. It is generally best to move as quickly as possible.

EXAMPLE:
• A buyer bid $250,000 on an apartment, but the seller refused to go below $275,000, and the buyer wanted time to think. The salesperson said: "Sure, take some time. Some other people are interested in the apartment. Maybe one of them will bid $275,000, or if there are no offers, the seller may become more flexible. Take your time, and I'll let you know." The buyer increased her offer right away.

The moral of the story: Every day a deal sits on the shelf is a day closer to its becoming rotten.

🎵 CONTROLLING YOUR DEAL

In most negotiations someone leads and someone follows. The leadership role can be powerful. You want to be in a position to keep things moving and make the deal happen. To lead, you must identify the decisions to be made and propose answers. If you do, your ideas will be the basis for deciding what to do.

EXAMPLES:

• A buyer was thinking about purchasing an apartment with an asking price of $350,000. When the salesperson asked, "How would you like to proceed?" the buyer said he wanted to think about it. The salesperson said: "Give me $300,000. I think I can make that deal." The buyer agreed.

• My partner, Marc, and I were buying a building. Our attorney, Louis Gotthelf, had been in the real estate business for more than 40 years and was considered one of the best. The seller was also using a reputable and established attorney. However, when the seller's attorney sent the contract over to Mr. Gotthelf, he turned beet red. He got on the phone and started yelling: "How dare you send me this contract! This is an outrage!" The seller's attorney apologized: "Lou, I didn't know you were representing those guys. I'll send you over the good contract right away. I'm sorry."

The moral of the story: If you are a leader, others will listen to what you have to say.

❧ SUMMARY

You have already learned the fundamentals of selling. This chapter gives you some extra strategies and refinements. Authority, Consistency, Affinity, Reciprocity, Exclusivity, Scarcity and Social Proof (A CARESS) are discussed in more detail, and examples are given of their use in negotiations. The techniques I call Quicksand, Diplomacy,

And Yet, Fait Accompli, Good Guy/Bad Guy, Price vs. Terms, Persuasive Words, Create an Auction, Clarity, Time and Controlling Your Deal are also explored.

ROBERT: *"Can you briefly describe what each of the negotiating terms means?"*

AUTHORITY: Someone perceived as knowledgeable can greatly influence decision-making.

CONSISTENCY: A customer desires to remain true to his logic, values or beliefs. The customer's yearning to stay consistent can be a powerful tool for persuasion.

AFFINITY: A relationship with the customer or identified commonality of interests will help you be persuasive.

RECIPROCITY: We all share the concept that agreements should be fair. A concession on one side invites a corresponding concession from the other.

EXCLUSIVITY: We want what many desire yet few can obtain.

SCARCITY: Limited supply heightens demand. If buyers are in limited supply, sellers must be flexible and vice versa.

SOCIAL PROOF: The customer will want others whose views he cares about to approve of his decision.

QUICKSAND: Events can be manipulated to draw you into a bad deal with no way out.

DIPLOMACY: Try to develop consensus. Achieving agreement on small issues can create momentum that leads to overall success.

AND YET: Either silence or pointed questions can be very persuasive.

FAIT ACCOMPLI: Defining side issues as "facts" can reduce the number of issues that need to be negotiated.

GOOD GUY/BAD GUY: Acting with a partner (or using corporate policy as the "bad guy") permits you to be sympathetic and still demand concessions. You can have disagreement without personal anger.

PRICE VS. TERMS: A customer who is inflexible about price may give concessions on the terms, including the time and method of payment.

PERSUASIVE WORDS: Words like "equal," "fair" and "just" create a conciliatory environment, encouraging flexibility and agreement.

CREATE AN AUCTION: When a sale becomes a competition, no one wants to lose.

CLARITY: Certain techniques can help you identify the crucial elements of a deal. If you concentrate on the fundamentals, peripheral issues often resolve themselves.

TIME: Keep a deal moving quickly toward consummation.

CONTROLLING YOUR DEAL: If you initiate proposals, you control the topic of discussion and the basis for resolution.

❧

Dealing with an Unfair World

ONE SUMMER YEARS AGO, I TOOK A SHARE IN A GROUP HOUSE IN WESTHAMPTON BEACH ON LONG ISLAND. THERE WERE GENERALLY 10 OF US WHO ARRIVED ON FRIDAY EVENINGS EAGER FOR A WEEKEND OF HOOPLA, BUT GROUP MEMBERS OCCASIONALLY BROUGHT FRIENDS ALONG TO ADD TO THE FESTIVITIES.

WE ASSIGNED OURSELVES TASKS: SOME WOULD SHOP, SOME WOULD COOK AND SOME WOULD CLEAN UP AFTER MEALS. ALL GROUP MEMBERS CONTRIBUTED TOWARD FOOD AND STAPLES.

SOME MINOR ISSUES DEVELOPED. I, FOR ONE, DIDN'T LIKE THE FOOD SELECTED BY THE SHOPPERS. THEY PREFERRED TOFU AND SALADS, WHILE I CRAVED JUNK FOOD AND DELI MEATS. WE AGREED THAT WE COULD EACH PURCHASE ADDITIONAL FOOD AT OUR OWN EXPENSE AND KEEP IT IN A SEPARATE COMPARTMENT IN THE REFRIGERATOR.

ONE DAY I WENT TO THE REFRIGERATOR TO GET MY SLICED ROAST BEEF. AS SOON AS I PLACED THE PACKAGE ON THE KITCHEN COUNTER, HOWEVER, A GUEST CAME INTO THE KITCHEN, LOOKED AT ME STERNLY AND SAID, "WHAT ARE YOU DOING?" I ASKED, "WHAT DO YOU MEAN?" HE SAID: "DON'T YOU SEE THE BREAD ON THAT PLATE? THAT'S MY BREAD, AND YOU ARE TAKING THE ROAST BEEF I WAS GOING TO USE FOR MY SANDWICH!" HE GRABBED THE ROAST BEEF, PUT IT ON HIS PLATE AND WALKED OUT INTO THE BACKYARD.

MY FRIEND WHO OBSERVED ALL OF THIS WAS SHOCKED. "WHAT'S THE MATTER WITH YOU?" HE SAID. "YOU JUST LET THAT GUY TAKE YOUR ROAST BEEF!" I SAID: "AT THE BEGINNING OF THE SUMMER, I ALLOCATED $200 FOR INJUSTICE. SO FAR I'VE USED VERY LITTLE OF IT, SO I'M WAY AHEAD OF THE GAME."

My friend was aghast, and said: "That's ridiculous! It isn't fair." I said: "If the world were fair it would be boring; I like not knowing what will happen. Besides, unfairness is a reality. I would rather prepare for it than get angry about it."

CHAPTER 14

&

The Basic Principles of Selling

It does not matter whether you are selling a product, service or idea — these principles will help you succeed.

THE FOUR ROLES IN SELLING

To sell, you must master four roles. The first is the *Personality Role*, in which you consciously choose which "you" to be in order to connect effectively with your unique customer. Don't go on autopilot; think about which aspects of your personality will help you build rapport. If you step into a personality the customer likes, you will be the person he wants to talk to. Choose consciously.

Keep the objective of building rapport with your customer firmly in mind. See his point of view, even if it is not yours. Adopt his point of view for the purpose of understanding how to accommodate his needs. Don't worry if you must pretend: to the mind, everything is real.

Second is the *Authority Role*, in which you establish legitimacy. If the customer views your information as apropos and credible, he will value and appreciate your input. Present your information in a way that is structured, concise and meaningful so the customer understands his choices and can compare different alternatives. If you lead him out of confusion and into clarity, you will be able to influence his thinking. First understand his needs, then show him how to fulfill his goals.

Third is the *Projection Role*, in which you envision the path to the customer's objective. If you have foreseen and prepared for the obstacles, the journey will be easier and the objective more easily achieved.

You understand your customer by Switching, trying on his psychological clothing, rather than Shifting, or attributing your beliefs to him [*Chapter 10*]. Do the visualization exercise in Chapter 7 and "step into" the customer. Go all the way — become the customer. The Projection Role will help you to gain awareness and understanding.

The final role is *Mediation*, in which you resolve different points of view. At first the path to your goal is dark, but information provides light. As the darkness fades, new opportunities for consensus and agreement appear. You must illuminate the various points of view with information, find the overlap of goals between the buyer and the seller and eliminate the darkness of disagreement.

Think of your four roles — Personality, Authority, Projection and Mediation — as a row of switches. If energy enters the circuit and all the switches are on, a bulb lights up. If any of the switches is off, the bulb stays dark. If you are not selling effectively, one of your switches may be off. To find which one, try something different. It doesn't matter if what you try is right or wrong — any change will give you feedback that will reveal new choices for moving forward. Look for an answer. It need not be the right answer — that will come later.

∾ UNDERSTANDING THE UNDERLYING PRINCIPLES OF EFFECTIVE SELLING

Certain principles underlie the process of selling. The acronym BUFF-PIC will help you remember them.

"B" STANDS FOR BIO-COMPUTER. Like a computer, your customer acts predictably according to a program based on his experience. To communicate effectively, you must understand the program rules and input data in a way that will get through.

"U" STANDS FOR UNIQUENESS. Each customer is unique; no two people can be relied upon to act the same way.

"F" STANDS FOR FLEXIBILITY. Look at any problem from the broadest possible viewpoint, and don't get overcommitted to a solution that isn't working. The salesperson that offers the most choices will be able to lead most effectively — he will always have an alternative to suggest when a particular path proves unproductive.

"F" STANDS FOR FAILURE, which is a label placed on an event that could as easily be viewed as a positive. Failures are sources of information that can be critical for making more informed decisions later. Failure is a necessary step toward success.

"P" STANDS FOR PERFECT. People make decisions that are perfect according to the information they have at that time. New information will cause them to reconsider.

"I" STANDS FOR INFORMATION, which is the essential element of any negotiation. Decisions change when additional information reveals better alternatives.

"C" STANDS FOR CONTROL. You control the outcome of the sale. The responsibility and the opportunity lie with you.

Keep Your Eye on the Prize

PRESIDENT LINCOLN WAS FRUSTRATED BY THE INABILITY OF HIS GENERALS TO TAKE EFFECTIVE COMMAND OF THE UNION ARMY. HE HIRED AND FIRED ONE AFTER ANOTHER, BUT NONE SHOWED THE RIGHT DETERMINATION AGAINST THE CONFEDERATE FORCES. FINALLY, GENERAL ULYSSES S. GRANT SCORED A GREAT UNION VICTORY IN VICKSBURG, MISSISSIPPI. WHEN A GROUP OF CITIZENS COMPLAINED THAT GRANT WAS A DRUNK-ARD AND INCOMPETENT AND SHOULD BE RELIEVED OF HIS COM-MAND, A GRATIFIED LINCOLN REPLIED: "THIS MAN FIGHTS. FOR THE FIRST TIME, I HAVE A GENERAL WHO LEADS HIS MEN TO VIC-TORY, AND YOU COMPLAIN THAT HE DRINKS! TELL ME WHAT LABEL OF WHISKEY HE PREFERS SO I MIGHT SEND HIM A CASE."

GRANT LED THE UNION ARMY TO VICTORY AFTER VICTORY UNTIL HE ACCEPTED GENERAL ROBERT F. LEE'S SURRENDER AT APPOMATTOX ON APRIL 9, 1865 — THE WAR WAS WON.

Conclusion

To apply the strategy I have set forth, you need not climb a mountain, straining with every step. I see a different picture: You are walking down a dirt road on a beautiful sunny day. As you walk, you see a stone. You pick it up, noticing its texture and color, and put it in your pocket. You notice other interesting stones and hold on to them as well. Each one you pick up is a bit of knowledge. Each is a jewel of great value to be kept as a precious resource while you walk down the road of your life.

I love to read biographies of great people. They all struggled against long odds and experienced failure, and naysayers impeded their progress, but in the end they triumphed. Greatness was found in log cabins, basements and garages. Wisdom appeared in the darkest part of the night. However, each breakthrough took time to form. A path was chosen and followed — one step at a time until "overnight success" followed years of preparation and thoughtful work.

Now it is your turn. Take the first step toward your destination. Begin deliberately down your own path.

Take one chapter of this book and use it today. Test it with a friend. Explore it with a customer. See what happens. If it doesn't work, ask yourself why and come up with your own ideas. Look at it as a stone that you are studying. Consider its color and texture and identify its beauty. Then place the stone in your pocket and continue. The ideas are yours to keep and use.

What if you learned something that made a difference? You may sell more. You may persuade more. Your thoughts may influence other people's actions. You may become a wiser and more successful person in more ways than you ever imagined.

(Blank)

(Blank)